Various types of Bonsai

双幹 "Sō-kan" (twine trunks)

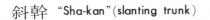

斜幹 "Sha-kan" (slanting trunk)

蟠幹 "Ban-kan" (crooked or twisted trunk)

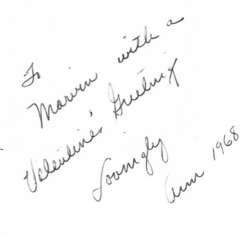

BONSAI

MINIATURE POTTED TREES

by

Kyuzo Murata

SHUFUNOTOMO CO., LTD.

Tokyo, Japan

...ed Pine) **in a Rock·**
...le **in front of the**

...pure stream. The
..., one to the right,
...d to the right fore-
... The whole is a
...th and 3 meters
in length.   The bonsai of *Goyō-Matsu* (Five-Needled Pine) which is placed in the middle represents a pine-tree growing on a rock. The tree is about 100 years old. It belongs to a rare variety with rough bark. The container is light brown in color. The rock in the foreground is a red rock produced in the province of Tamba.

Publisher
SHUFUNOTOMO PUBLISHING CO., LTD.

6, 1-chome, Kanda Surugadai
Chiyodaku, Tokyo, Japan

Exclusive Distributors
JAPAN PUBLICATIONS TRADING CO., LTD.

Central P.O. Box 722, Tokyo, Japan

Printed in Japan

Goyo-Matsu (Five-Need
Garden of Japanese Sty
Main Entrace

The pebbles symbolize a
three rocks of various size
one to the left, and the thir
ground symbolize a valley.
rock garden 1 meter in wid

Zaifuri-boku (Japanese Juneberry

This is a deciduous tree found in
tains. The plant is beautiful to
spring at budding-time, in autu
leaves change color, and even a

2

Iwa-Shide (Carpinus Turczaninovii Hance). 'Kabudachi'—Multi-trunk Style.

The shape of the tree gives an image of a huge tree, well taken care of. It is a tree such as one might see in a park. About 100 years old. 70 years since it was planted in the container.

Aka-Ezo-Matsu (Saghalien Spruce) "Sha-kan" Slanting Trunk Style.

The shape of the tree suggests that of a huge tree in nature. The lower branches have a color that suggests great age. 120 years old.

Shimpaku (Chinese Juniper). "Moyogi". Plant which has a gnarled trunk.

The main trunk is a natural trunk without any artificial treatment. The branches, however, have been arranged. 400 years old. 40 years since it was planted in the container.

Sugi (Japanese Cedar). "Chokkan" Single Straight Trunk Style.

This is a "bonsai" made from a tree found in the mountains. Most 'Sugi' (Japanese Cedar) are trees obtained from the top of a

Sugi

tree by the process of layering. 80 years old.

Soro (*Aka-Shide*) (Loose-flower Hornbeam). "Yose-ue", several plants planted together. The appearance of the tree suggests a grove in winter. The container is elliptical, and the tree is planted in such a way as to create the illusion of a gentle basin. About 20 years old.

Soro

To-Kaede (Trident Maple). Bonsai planted on a rock.

This is a rare type in which the tree grows from the side of a rock. Ordinarily, the tree is planted on top of a rock. 70 years old. 50 years since it was planted on the rock.

Goyo-Matsu (Five-Needled Pine) Planted on a flat rock. "Netsuranari" the roots of the trees are connected.

This tree has been uprooted from the mountains. Planted on a flat rock, water drains easily, and the plant is easy to grow. This method is very popular as bonsai in Japan. 60 years old.

To-Kaede

Yabai (*Ume*) (Variety of Flowering Japanese Apricot). "Chokkan" Single Straight Trunk Style.

'Ume' (Flowering Japanese Apricot) which bursts into bloom in cold weather is a symbol of nobility. Half of the trunk is decayed. Fresh-green 'Mame-Zuta' (Drymoglossum microplyblum C. Chi.) is seen on the trunk. 150 years old.

Buna (Japanese Beech). "Yose-ue" several plants planted together.

This is the technique of creating the appearance of a forest of 'Buna' spreading to the left and right from the miniature center. 30 years old.

Zakuro (Pomergranate) "Moyogi." (Plant which has a gnarled trunk).

This tree has been obtained from the tip of a tree in the garden by layering. Its fruits are particularly beautiful in summer and autumn. However, if the tree is allowed to bear too many fruits, withering of branches may set in. 20 years old.

Kuma-Shide (Carpinus carpinoides) "Moyogi" (Plant which has a gnarled trunk) The fruits are at first green, but when the leaves fall, they turn brown. The manner in which the fruits fall in the wind is particularly beautiful. 60 years old.

Yabai

Goyo-Matsu

Buna

Zakuro

Kuma-Shide

HOW TO OBTAIN TREES BY LAYERING.

In spring, choose a strong young tree about 10 to 20 years old. Peel off the bark in the form of a ring about 3 cm. in width from its forked trunk or branch. Tie sphagnum-moss around the place where it was peeled and give water daily. In about a year, the branch is ready to become a separate tree. This method make it possible to obtain several trees for *bonsai* from one tree.

(1) When the roots have developed to such an extent that they stick out of the sphagnum moss, cut off the branch.

Plant the tree in a container still with the sphagnum-moss on and grow for about a year, determining each part of the tree as (2) the top, (3) the central part, and (4) the lower part. The soil should be sifted so that it will both drain and hold water well.

(5) After two years, remove the tree from the container for growing and transplant it in a container for *bonsai*.

Photograph (3) shows the tree as it has been removed from the container. Remove the soil carefully with a stick so as not to injure the roots. Also remove the sphagnum-

moss which was used in the process of layering. (6) Six months after the plant has been planted in the container, roots will fill up the container. The photograph shows the roots after a year. The trunk which appears at the lower part should be cut off from the base near the roots. The trunk which has appeared in the upper part may either be cut off or be made to assume the shape of a decayed branch. Cut off one third of the total length of the roots.

(7) Cover the hole at the bottom of the container for *bonsai* by means of a plastic net. The lid of a tin can, if perforated with many holes, may be used.

(8) A mixture of the basic soil should be put in after sifting.

(9) Place the tree in the container, then put in some more soil, making sure that the soil penetrates the fine roots. To ensure this, use a stick.

(10) After all the soil has been put in, press it down lightly with a trowel.

(11) After the tree has been planted, give water until it flows out of the hole at the bottom of the container. Place the container where the sun shines only in the morning. Be sure that it is not exposed to any strong winds. After two or three days, give water as you would to any other plant.

When a tree is obtained by layering from a tree that is, say, 20 years old, it will be possible to enjoy viewing the *bonsai* in about three years as if it were a tree 20 or 30 years old. The photographs show, from left to right, a *bonsai* of 'Aka-Ezo-Matsu' (Saghalien Spruce) obtained by layering after 3 years, 4 years, 5 years, 10 years, 12 years and finally 18 years, when the tree has achieved perfect form as *bonsai*.

HOW TO TRANSPLANT BONSAI

(1) The photograph shows 'Shimpaku' (Chinese Juniper) that has not been transplanted for 5 years. It has been taken out of the container. There is almost no soil left. The time for transplanting should be some time in spring when the temperature is about 18 degrees Centigrade.

(2) Remove the old soil and untangle the root system.

(3) Prune all overgrown roots. Cut off about 1/3 of the entire length the roots.

(4) Cover the hole at the bottom of the container, and put in large clods of soil at the bottom.

(5) Put the plant in and determine its position in the container. Fasten the tree in the container by inserting a plastic string through the hole at the bottom. Do not use any copper wire, as copper wire may rust and harm the roots.

(6) Put in the soil mixture.

(7) Make sure that the soil penetrates the root system. To ensure this use a stick.

(8) Press the soil down gently with a trowel. Apply water until it flows out of the hole at the bottom of the container. Place the container where the sun shines only in the morning. Avoid exposure to a strong wind. Give the plant in normal quantities after two or three days.

12

CONTENTS

PREFACE

The art of *Bonsai*, together with the Japanese flower-arrangement, *Ikebana*, has been originated in Japan and are now being admired throughout the world. Among the lovers and admirers of *Bonsai*, there are many who find an infinite pleasure in growing *Bonsai*—a satisfaction of creating by their own hands the beauty of nature in miniature. Although there are several publications on *Bonsai*, very few books have been published for the beginners.

This book has as its objective the explanation of the art from the very start for the benefit of those who wish to launch upon the growing of *Bonsai*. And to achieve the objective photographs and illustrations are included as many as possible with a hope to render a complete and comprehensive explanation. There are various methods of growing *Bonsai*. The quick way is to dig out a plant in the garden or uprooting a young wild tree in the forest and plant it in the container. Then there are other ways such as arranging the branches by wiring, forming the shape of tree to suit one's taste. The book intends to render a practical help to all those who desire to grow *Bonsai* from an available tree, emphasizing the growing techniques as well as the pleasure of viewing the plant as *Bonsai*.

The growing of *Bonsai* gives the grower an enjoyment that lasts throughout the year round—a pleasure which can not be obtained in growing flowers in the garden. *Bonsai* changes with the seasons. And as it grows older, it exhibits more and more the beauty of trees found in nature. And this pleasure, the author wishes to share with as many people as possible.

Kyuzo Murata
October, 1964

ANSWERS TO QUESTIONS
CONCERNING THE ART OF *BONSAI*

What is *Bonsai*?

Bonsai consist of trees or bushes, and sometimes of perennial herbs found in fields and mountains, which are artistically planted in small pot or container, occasionally in combination with rocks of many forms, so as to reproduce in miniature the lordly appearance of large aged trees or landscape such as found in nature. Hence they are quite different from ordinary potted plants whose primary purpose is the enjoyment of their leaves and blossoms.

The art of *bonsai* originates with the Japanese, lovers of gardening, and it may be considered the highest form of horticulture as a hobby. In fact, *bonsai* of the best kind can be fully appreciated, much as painting or sculpture, for their elegance as a plastic art. Even if such heights cannot be attained, the pleasure of growing *bonsai* is unique, and its decorative purposes, both in the garden and indoors, make it an art that yields lasting enjoyment.

Kuro-Matsu (Japanese Black Pine) which reproduces the appearance of a huge old tree in miniature.

Sasa (Small Bamboo) and *Aka-Ezo-Matsu* (Saghalien Spruce) planted on a flat rock to represent natural landscape in miniatuee.

What are the elements that make *Bonsai*?

The three elements of *bonsai* are: (1) The containers in which the trees are planted; (2) The soil; and (3) The plants which are grown in the containers. Of these three elements, the first two, namely the containers and the soil put therein, represent the earth, and the plants represent the herbs, bushes, and trees that grow on the earth. In addition to the plants, if rocks are used, they serve as auxiliary natural features.

Hence, it follows naturally that the containers and soil used must both be of such a kind as will be favorable to the growth of plants. However, containers which are too large, filled with a great quantity of soil, tend to take up more space than desirable. Their handling also becomes a problem. It is for this reason that the containers must be no larger than would make it possible for a single person to move them freely. Again, the plant to be grown as *bonsai* must be of such a species as will allow it to grow within this restricted space and yet exhibit all its characteristics when in the natural state. To this end, the plant chosen must be of a dwarf-nature or one that lends itself to grow-

ing up as a miniature plant.

Kaki (Japanese Persimmon) which shows in a small container all the qualities of the tree in its normal state.

17

What are the necessary conditions of *Bonsai* ?

As necessary conditions of *bonsai,* the following six may be listed:

(1) The plant used as *bonsai* in a container must have all the vitality of a living plant. Moreover, must it terminate in the top which indicates the highest point of its growth.

(2) The trunk near the roots and the main trunk above the ground must have all the aspects of natural growth, in addition to the appearance of age, characteristic of large trees that are several decades old.

(3) The branches must be rich in variety and of artistic appearance.

(4) There must be perfect harmony between the shape of the container and the appearance of the trees or herbs therein planted, so that the over-all effect will be one of stability.

(5) The plants chosen must be of such species as exhibit all the variations that accompany the changes of the seasons, so that they will yield enjoyment to the eye all year round.

(6) Since all *bonsai*-growers value nature, the plants must be so chosen that they will betray only the minimum of artificiality.

Goyo-Matsu (Five-Needled Pine), masterpiece with two trunks.

What are the merits of *Bonsai*?

The purpose of *bonsai* has always been the appreciation of the total appearance of the plant. However, in viewing *bonsai*, the following points deserve attention as special merits:

(1) In the case of a single tree:
  (a) The condition of the rootage, how the main roots strike into the earth;
  (b) The appearance of the trunk as it rises above the ground;
  (c) The curvature of the trunk;
  (d) The rugged appearance of the bark, creating an illusion of great age;
  (e) The artistic appearance of the branches;
  (f) The shape and color of the leaves, as well as their changes in accordance with the seasons;
  (g) The blossoms and fruits, together with all their variations of shape and color;
  (h) The position and size of the top;
  (i) The condition of the mosses that cover the surface of soil.

(2) In the case of trees and herbs planted together, in addition to the foregoing:
  (a) The girth and length of the trunks;
  (b) Curvature and the sense of perspective.

Keyaki (Zelkova), one of the famous trees of Keyaki bonsai.

(3) In the case of herbs found in plains and mountains:
  (a) The distribution of the plants;
  (b) The condition of the blossoms and fruits, and their color arrangement.

What kind of plants are fitted for *Bonsai*?

Approximately 3,000 species or varieties of plants are found in the territory of Japan which extends from the subtropics to the sub-frigid zone. Of this number, roughly half are unfit for growing as *bonsai*. However, about 40% of the total vegetation are trees, and of this number, nearly 80% can be used for purposes of *bonsai*.

Particularly among the so-called conifers, including the various species of pine-trees, such as Ezo-Matsu (Saghalien Spruce), Shimpaku (Chinese Juniper), Sugi (Japanese Cedar), Tosho (Needle Juniper), etc., there are many that have the dwarf-nature and easily lend themselves to growing as miniature plants or *bonsai*. Actually, however, young trees suitable for *bonsai* have all but been

Aka-Ezo-Matsu (Saghalien Spruce), young plant grown by cutting.

completely taken away from their native places, with the result that growing from seeds, cutting, grafting, layering, and other forms of artificial reproduction methods must be used at present to meet the demand for *bonsai* plants.

Sugi (Japanese Ceder) grown by wiring and pinching.

In contrast to this situation in Japan, America with its territory many times larger than the whole of Japan, and enjoying varying climates, must be a veritable treasury of plants with its fields and mountains of virgin land. There must be an inexhaustible supply of *bonsai* plants there if only one takes the trouble to look.

What are some rules that *Bonsai*-growers must bear in mind?

(1) *The young plant must be planted in a small container.* If one finds a plant that seems suitable for growing as *bonsai,* whether it is a tree or a perennial herb, it should be dug out of the soil or purchased from the dealer, planted in a small container from which water drains freely, given plentiful water, and placed in semi-shade with weak sunlight.

(2) *The young plant should be placed on an outdoor shelf and be watered.* After the plant has developed roots, it should be placed on an airy outdoor shelf. (Care should be taken not to place *bonsai* directly on the ground.) The plant should be exposed to plentiful sunlight. However, each time the surface of the soil in the container becomes dry, water should be applied without fail.

(3) *Care.* Fertilizer should be given from time to time. New buds should be pinched just about the time the leaves take definite shape. Of course, all insects and pests should be removed, and in winter, proper protective measures must be taken to prevent the soil in the container from freezing.

(4) *Transplanting.* Transplanting should be done once in every one to two years' time. It should be done in spring just before the new sprouts come out.

If these rules are faithfully observed in the care of plants, in a few years, some of them will begin to develop all the aspects of a *bonsai* in the true sense of the term, and may even bear blossoms or fruits, depending on the species.

Aren't *Bonsai* a great deal of trouble?

Of course, there is no end to the care that may be bestowed on *bonsai.* Still, all in all, *bonsai* require less attention than flowers grown in pots. Especially after one has acquired the knack of tending *bonsai,* giving water when dryness of the soil requires it, applying fertilizer before it is exhausted, pinching the buds when they have grown oversize, etc., the work required is not so time-consuming if these operations are performed with proper timing. Much needless labor can be eliminated, and moreover, the results can be quite satisfactory. In one word, the art of *bonsai* growing is one that requires only the minimum of trouble if only one masters the technique.

However, it must be borne in mind that *bonsai* are plants planted, not in the ground, but in small pots, so that their care has certain rigid requirements as to time. If there is no one to look after them all through the year, or if they can be looked after only on Sundays, success in this art could be extremely difficult.

How many years does it take to make a *Bonsai*?

Of course, the actual number of years required for a given plant to develop into a *bonsai* depends on a multitude of factors, such as species, the technique of developing its form and arranging its branches, the environment, the care given to the plant, the ability of the grower, etc. The following list gives the average number of years required for each plant respectively:

Years required	Species	Materials	Planting	Remarks
1—2 years	*Kusa-boke* (Maule's Quince)	Young plant taken from the mountains	Several plants planted together	Only plants with good branches and blossoms should be used
3 years	*Miyama-Kirishima-Tsutsuji* (Rhododendron Kiusianum)	From cutting liner 1—2 years	Single plant	Container should be 12 cm in diameter. Buds should be pinched to keep the plant compact.
5—6 years	*Tsubaki* (Garden Camellia)	Seedling of 1 year	Single plant	Main stem should be pruned to keep plant about 30 cm. in height. Branches should be developed, and the plant be made to bear blossoms.
5—6 years	*Yamagaki* (Wild Japanese Persimmon)	Grafted plant of 1 year	Single plant	For the original plant, a persimmon should be grafted on to a persimmon seedling of 2 years.
5—6 years	*Ume* (Japanese Apricot)	Seedling of 4—5 years	Single plant	First the plant should be grown in the garden and its branches pruned each year.
5—6 years	*Beni-Shitan* (Cotoneaster horizontalis)	1 or 2 year liner from cutting	Single plant	Main stem should be pruned to keep the plant about 20 cm, in height. Branches should be developed, and the plant be made to bear berries.
7—8 years	*Aka-Ezo-Matsu* (Saghalien Spruce); *Shimpaku* (Chinese Juniper)	Plant propagated by layering, or cutting of 3 years	Single plant	Buds should be frequently pinched to arrange branches.
7—8 years	*Keyaki* (Zelkova-tree); *Soro*; (Lose-flower Hornbeam) *Momiji* (Maple); *Kaede* (Maple)	Seedling of 1 year	Single plant or several planted together	
10 years	*Kuro-Matsu* (Japanese Black Pine); *Goyomatsu* (Five-Needled Pine)	Young plant taken from the mountains	Single plant or several planted together	New buds should be closely pinched, and the branches should be properly arranged by wiring.
15 years and above	*Akamatsu* (Japanese Red Pine)	Seedling of 1 year	Single plant	

How many years do *Bonsai* last?

The age of a *bonsai* depends on the species and the care given it. However, with the exception of the bamboo species which are short-lived (7–8 years at most), there are few that wither within 50 years. With proper care given at the proper time, all other species last from 60–70 years, and some even several centuries. Particularly the pine species, in addition to Ume (Japanese Apricot), Boke (Japanese Quince), Momiji (Maple), To-kaede (Trident Maple), Keyaki (Zelkova-tree), Buna (Japanese Beech), Karin (Chinese Quince), etc., last so long that their life-span is beyond speculation.

Ume (Flowering Japanese Apricot) which has been grown for 70 to 80 years.

GUIDE TO GROWING *BONSAI*

Start with cheaper trees.

As stated before, a *bonsai* is quite different from an ordinary potted plant. It is advisable not to spend too much money at the start, until the important techniques of caring have fairly been mastered.

Of course, by purchasing a fully developed *bonsai* one can enjoy viewing from the very next day. However, such a *bonsai* is expensive in the first place and it is not so easy to take care of it, or to maintain it in a healthy and original condition.

So anyone who wishes to enjoy the art of *bonsai* should start with his own hands by following the *bonsai* growing techniques stated heretofore by purchasing a healthy young tree for growing as *bonsai* for a dollar or two. And with a meticulous care for a year or two it is possible to master the method of *bonsai* growing. From then on he should proceed to more advanced levels step by step. This procedure may be termed the safest and soundest way of mastering the art of *bonsai*.

Goyo-matsu (Five-needled Pine) which is hardy and easy to grow.

Kind of plants suitable for beginners.

The following plants are deemed suitable for beginners of *bonsai*.

(1) Conifers or needle-leafed evergreens— 'Kuro-Matsu' (Japanese Black Pine), 'Goyo-Matsu' (Five-Needled Pine), 'Aka-Ezo-Matsu' (Saghalien Spruce), Sugi (Japanese Cedar), 'Tosho' (Needle Juniper), 'Shimpaku' (Chinese Juniper) are suited for enjoying both the leaves and the general appearance of the tree.

(2) Broad-leafed Evergreens—'Kuchinashi' (Cape Gardenia), 'Tsubaki' (Camellias), 'Sazanka' (Sasanqua), 'Cha' (Tea-plant) are suited for enjoying both the flowers and the general appearance of the plant.

(3) Small-leafed evergreens—'Beni-Shitan' (Rock Cotoneaster), 'Tachibanamodoki' (Narrow-leaf Firethorn) are suited for enjoying both the berries and the general appearance of the plant.

(4) Deciduous trees—'Ume' (Flowering Japanese Apricot), 'Boke' (Japanese Quince), 'Sanzashi' (Chinese Hawthorn), 'Kaido' (Showy Crab Apple), 'No-bara' (Japanese Dog Rose), 'Kirishima-Tsutsuji' (Kirishima Azalea), 'Satsuki' (Satsuki Azalea), 'Sarusuberi' or 'Hyakujikko' (Crape Myrtle) are suited for enjoying both the flowers and the general appearance of the tree. 'Momiji' (Japanese Maple), 'To-kaede' (Trident Maple), 'Keyaki' (Zelkova), 'Buna' (Japanese Beech), 'Soro' (Loose-Flower Hornbeam), 'Tsuta' (Japanese Ivy) are suited for enjoying both the leaves and the general appearance of the plant. 'Yusura-Ume' (Prunus Tomentosa Thunb) is suited for enjoying the flowers, fruits, and the general appearance of the tree. 'Gumi' (Elaeagnus), 'Hime-Ringo' (Nagasaki Crab Apple), 'Karin' (Chinese Quince), 'Umemodoki' (Ilex Serrata, var. Cieboldii), 'Kuko' (Boxthorn) are suited for enjoying the fruits and the general appearance of the tree.

Fire Thorn (left), *Shimpaku* (Chinese Juniper) (center), and *Beni-Shitan* (Rock Cotoneaster) (right), all of which are hardy and easy to grow.

Satsuki (Satsuki Azalea) which is easy to grow and bears particularly beautiful flowers.

Momiji (Japanese Maple) which is prized for its autumnal tints and also for the appearance of the tree in winter.

Karin (Chinese Quince) which is prized for its hardiness and long life, as well as beauty of appearance.

Method of choosing a practicing-tree.

The above are the varieties of trees which can be easily obtained and are easy to grow as practicing-trees whether it is a young tree or one being grown for *bonsai*. However, in choosing the following factors should be kept in mind.

Suitable season Begin in a season when plants can be easily transported without inflicting damage in transplanting. For example, in the case of:

(a) Needle-leafed evergreens: The months of October and November or during spring budding.

(b) Evergreen broad-leafed trees: During spring budding or the period of maturing of young leaves.

(c) Small-leafed evergreens: During spring budding.

(d) Deciduous trees: After the leaves have fallen in the warmer districts, and before spring budding in colder districts.

Choice of plant Although some difference is seen in plants being grown for *bonsai* and seedlings, in each case a plant should be selected which is low in height, has a strong trunk, thick near the roots. The ramifications of the roots must be as numerous as possible. The tree must have small and dense leaves, and free from injurious insects or diseases.

Of course, a tree with leaves which are beautiful throughout the four seasons is preferable. Furthermore, in the case of a plant which serves the dual purpose of enjoying the blossoms as well as the fruits, avoid such species with gorgeous and colorful flowers and fruits, and preference should be given to those whose flowers or fruits are elegant and tasteful.

Needles to say, plants with a fine arrangement of branches should be chosen. But it often happens, in the case of seedlings or trees grown by cutting or grafting for practice, that those without branches or those whose joints of grafting are too obvious are used. In the case of branchless seedlings, choice should be given to those in which the internode of the branches is short and which have healthy buds in the lower part. In the case of seedlings or cuttings whose roots are strong and which are grown too tall, the part exceding two-thirds of the height should be cut off. At the same time, the main root should be cut off as short as possible, keeping only the thicker part as it is. In the case of grafted trees, care should be taken to choose only such plants with perfect joints, and avoid those that show traces of unnatural joining.

The above are some important points not only in purchasing a plant, for practice but also in uprooting wild plants or in growing plants by grafting, cutting or by sowing seeds.

Container and soil preparation.

It is better if a tree is planted in the ground and grown for a year or two. This period allows the fine roots and branches to develop. In case a practicing-tree is a young tree or wild plant uprooted from a forest, it is better to plant it in the ground and give it fertilizer for a year or two. After the plant has grown strong with a good root system, thick branches and trunk, it is transplanted to a container, after pruning the roots and branches.

Planting directly in a container. However, often a plant is planted directly in the container without planting it in the ground first, so that care can be carried out thoroughly. With plants with reasonably goot root systems and leaves, there is no harm at all in planting them directly in a container.

Even in case a practicing-tree is already planted in a container, it is better to transplant it to examine whether it is properly planted, the soil is suitable and the roots

Various kinds of containers for growing *bonsai*.

are healthy. Before transplanting the container and the soil should be prepared.

Container The container should be a pot, inexpensive and unglazed or semi-hard baked pot suitable in shape and size and in balance with the size of the practicing plant, with good water drainage and retention. There is no need of using good glazed pottery from the very start. The container has a hole at the bottom for good aeration and water draining. Larger holes are preferable to prevent root decay.

A newly-purchased container should be washed thoroughly after immersing in water. When an old container is used, it should be only after thoroughly cleaning it, washing off soil, moss and disease germs.

The container should be used only after water is completely drained.

The soil Preference of soil differs with plants to some extent and also by country and by people. But the safest and productive soil has to have the following three characteristics:

(a) Good water retention and draining with good fertilizer absorption.

(b) Not containing too much fertilizer. (The composition and amount of fertilizer in soil can be ascertained only by analysis. Hence, it is better to use soil with little fertilizer at the beginning. Later, as the need arises, fertilizer should be supplied). The soil must be free from any disease germs or eggs or larvae of injurious insects.

(c) Acidity and alkali reaction of soil must not be strong. The soil should contain no poisonous substance injurious to plant growth.

However, natural soil satisfactorily meeting all of these three requirements is very rarely found. Therefore, soil of this type must be prepared by artificial mixing. The basic types of soil for mixing are herewith described:

Types and characteristics of basic soil The most widely used types of basic soil are as follows:

(a) *Kuro-tsuchi* (Black loam). This is the soil which is obtained from the lower strata of uplands. It is of a brownish-black color, and is soft clayey loam in character. It contains little fertilizer, is clean, holds water well

and absorbs fertilizer easily.

Not being sufficiently weathered, the hard lumps of this soil have the characteristic of not being broken up even after mixing with soil in the container. It is somewhat acid in quality. Any soil may be used so long as it has the same characteristics as black loam. However, if acidity is strong, the result will be the same as if too much fertilizer had been applied, and the leaves will turn yellow and ultimately fall without bearing any flowers or fruits.

(b) *'Aka-tsuchi'* (Red Clay). Red clay is found in highlands in and around Tokyo at a depth of 60 to 90 cm. It is reddish-brown and is a heavy clayey soil, having properties similar to those of black loam. Its lumps are hard to break, so that the soil both holds and drains water easily. Moreover, it does not convey to the roots of plants the effects of heat and cold. It also lends itself favorably to the growth of moss. (In *bonsai*, the growth of moss on the soil surface in the container is considered an additional beauty.) Because of these characteristics, red clay is considered one of the essential basic clay. In Japan, the soil most commonly used is red soil, but other types of soil, such as river or mountain sand, can also be used with equally satisfactory results.

(c) Coarse sand. Coarse sand consists of the broken fragments of rocks or stones. It is very rough and has many sharp edges. There are different varieties, such as mountain sand, river sand and sea sand. Of these, the kinds considered best suited for use as basic soil in Japan are Tenjin River sand, which belongs to the granite family, and 'Asama sand' and 'Kiryu sand,' belonging to the volcanic rock family.

(d) *'Kuro-boka.'* This is also called 'Poka soil.' It is the soil that forms the surface layer of uplands in the hilly districts of Tokyo. It is light, fine clayey loam and has a blackish color. It contains considerable amount of fertilizer, holds water well. and its fertilizer absorption is quite pronounced. However, because its particles are small and easily breakable, it does not drain off water so easily. Hence it should be mixed sparingly. It can be replaced by soil of a similar nature.

(e) *'Kanuma soil'*. This soil is said to be the product of the weathering process on volcanic rocks. It is found in the stratum beneath the top soil. It is very porous and consists of soft grains. When moist it turns a beautiful yellowish-brown color; when dry, a pale yellowish-white color. It also becomes light as ash when it is dry. The soil contains a very small amount of fertilizer and is clean with good water and fertilizer absorption. When it has absorbed too much water, it maintains the granular form a long time with good air and water permeability. It is fairly acid.

Preparation of basic soil. The basic soil should be dried separately in the sun. Then it should be classified by using large, medium and small sieves. The reason for drying is that, if the soil is moist, the sieves will become clogged and the sifting cannot be done satisfactorily. Again, if the soil consists of large and small grains, as is the case in the natural state, it is impossible to put it into a container, large grains at the bottom, medium grains in the middle, and small grains at the top. Moreover, if the grains are not properly sifted and arranged as just described, every time water or fertilizer is applied or rain falls, the fine grains will sink toward the bottom of the container jeopardizing air and water permeability so essential to the development of the root system and ultimately, root decay will set in.

Three kinds of sieves with 1.5 mm., 5 mm., and 12 mm. meshes should be prepared. The soil should first be sifted through a sieve with 1.5 mm. meshes so as to remove those fine particles that hamper water drainage. If these small particles are not removed, they will pack the soil as water is applied, and hamper its drainage. The soil is then sifted through a 6 mm. sieve to remove fine grains of earth. Lastly, it is passed through a 12 mm. sieve to remove medium grains of earth. The large grains of earth which remain in the sieve are put away in a separate place. The soil popularly called 'Kuro-dama-tsuchi' (Black round loam) or 'Aka-dama-tsuchi' (Red round clay) in Japan is obtained in this manner.

After the basic soil has been sifted and separated into three kinds, according to the

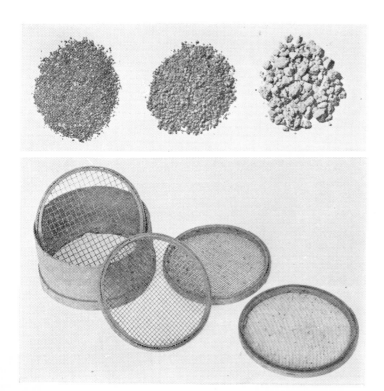

Various kinds of soil which has been sifted apart. From right, large lumps, medium lumps and small lumps.

One frame which can sift the soil into four different kinds according to size of the grains.

size of the grains of soil, large, medium and small respectively, the same should be put in separate boxes. Of these three kinds, the soil consisting of large grains is put at the bottom of the container to facilitate water drainage. Next, the soil consisting of medium grains is put in and the tree is planted. This type of soil promotes water drainage and is favorable to root growth. Lastly, the soil consisting of small grains is placed at the top to give the container a pleasing appearance. This soil need not be used always. The proportion with which the various kinds of soil must be mixed when the tree is to be planted in the container depends on the type of tree in question. (See the section on "Soil" in the chart 'Bonsai and their Care'.)

The soil which has been sifted and put in separate boxes should be placed indoors in a dry place, so that it will always be ready for use when need arises.

The technique of planting trees

Method of trimming roots and branches. A tree to be transplanted into a container for *bonsai* should not be watered from the previous day so that the soil in the container will be dry. The reason for this is to make it easier to remove the soil from the roots which have grown in the container. The next day, the side of the container should be struck with the fist two or three times to loosen the soil. The container should then be turned upside down, and the plant be removed from the container, soil and all, by pushing with the finger through the bottom hole.

Next, by means of a bamboo chopstick, about 1/3 of the old soil should be removed, care being taken not to injure the roots as

How to remove a plant from the container.

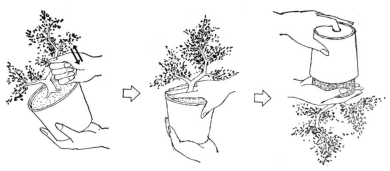

How to remove the old soil and cut the roots.

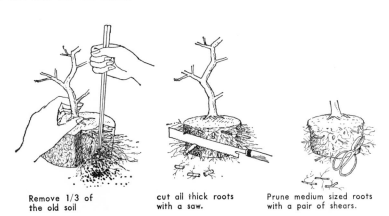

Remove 1/3 of the old soil

cut all thick roots with a saw.

Prune medium sized roots with a pair of shears.

shown in the illustration. Then about 1/3 of the thick root should be cut off with a pair of sharp shears. About 1/3 of the tips of the fine roots should also be cut off.

After the roots have thus been trimmed, the whole appearance of the tree should be considered, and if there are any parts where the branches are too close together, they should be cut off. If any branches have grown too long, they should be cut, too, to improve the general appearance of the tree. When a large branch has been cut off, the part that has been cut with a pair of shears should be smoothed over with a knife so as to ensure quicker healing.

In the case of a seedling, the root which has grown straight is already cut, so that the part cut should be smoothed in the same

How to prune the roots and branches of a young tree

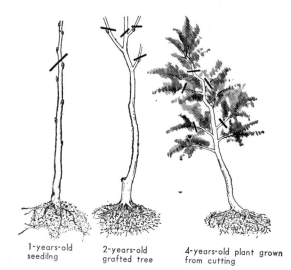

| 1-years-old seedilng | 2-years-old grafted tree | 4-years-old plant grown from cutting |

manner. If the root is still too long, it should be cut to fit the size of the container, the part cut being again smoothed. Care should be taken not to injure the fine roots by leaving the soil which is attached to them as it is.

As for the branches, only the tips of those that are too long should be cut off. But in the case of trees with few branches, no pruning should be done at all. In cutting off branches near the upper part of the trunk, the place to cut is where a healthy small branch or a bud is found. The cutting

should be done obliquely. The part cut shold be smoothed with a knife. In the case of 'Keyaki' (Zelkova), buds will appear anywhere on the branch, but in the case of 'Goyo-Matsu' (Five-Needled Pine), 'Kuro-Matsu' (Japanese Black Pine), or 'Ezo-Matsu' (Saghalien Spruce), buds appear only at certain places and at no other. In cutting, if the branch is thick and the part cut is consequently large, after smoothing with a knife, adhesive plaster or grafting wax should be applied. This prevents entry of rain water and also the drying of the wood part of the place cut, thus preventing decay.

Planting First of all, the container must be placed on the work table at a suitable height. If the table on which the container is placed can also be turned, so much the better. (See illustration.) Next, the hole at the bottom of the container should be covered with a fragment of a clay pot, or with a plastic net of 1.5 mm. mesh. This prevents the soil from dropping out of the container and also keeps the invasion of injurious insects through the hole. Next, put in soil consisting of large grains so as to facilitate water drainage. Then, put in soil consisting of medium grains. The tree is now ready for planning. It should be planted so as to present the best side to view, and it should also be planted right in the center of the container. Care should be taken not to plant the tree too deep, as this will conceal the base of the trunk where the roots spring. This part of the tree is one of the features of *bonsai*. In order not to conceal this part, the tree should be planted so that this part will be slightly above the edge of the container. The manner of the growth of the roots will then be clearly visible.

Next, soil consisting of medium grains should be put around the roots of the tree which has been planted. This soil should be put in small portions, in 3–4 applications, to fill the container up to about 3/4 of the whole vessel. As this soil is put in, it should be gently pounded with a bamboo chopstick to prevent the formation of empty spaces. Care should be taken, at the same time, not to apply too much pressure, as this hardens the soil and makes water drainage difficult, since the spaces created by the sifted medium

Steps and technique of planting a tree.

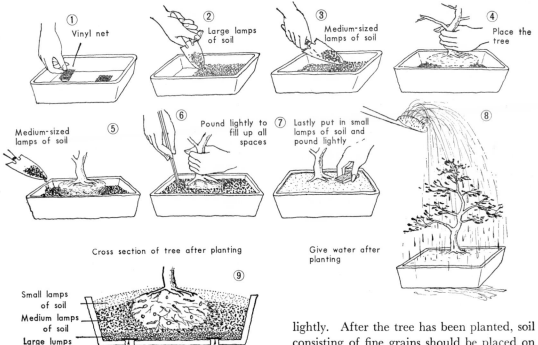

① Vinyl net

② Large lamps of soil

③ Medium-sized lamps of soil

④ Place the tree

⑤ Medium-sized lamps of soil

⑥ Pound lightly to fill up all spaces

⑦ Lastly put in small lamps of soil and pound lightly

⑧

Cross section of tree after planting

Give water after planting

⑨

Small lamps of soil
Medium lamps of soil
Large lumps of soil
Vinyl net

grains will be filled up completely. If the spaces are filled up, the water content increases unduly, and this is harmful to evergreens, many of which require not much water. Therefore, only the proper pressure should be applied. In the case of plants that bear flowers, fruits or leaves, the roots are fine, so the soil should be pressed down only lightly. After the tree has been planted, soil consisting of fine grains should be placed on the top to improve its general appearance. For this purpose, a flat trowel or a piece of wood might be used to press the soil down gently.

Water should be applied from the top of the plant by means of a watering can with a fine rose to moisten the whole tree. As soon as the water starts running out of the hole at the bottom of the container, the watering should be stopped.

Place for keeping the planted container.

The planted container should be placed for a week or two in a place where there is no wind, to assist the plant to take root properly. It should be exposed to the sunlight for two or three hours in the morning. During this period the plant should not be exposed to the cold or to heavy rain. It should be watered regularly to prevent the soil from drying. And it should not be brought into a room.

After this, the plant should be exposed to plenty of sunlight and air, preferably on a strong shelf built outdoors. However, during the summer, deciduous trees whose leaves might be burnt by the sunlight should be placed under a shed in the afternoon to keep it from exposure to the direct summer sunlight. In winter, deciduous trees, like 'Ume-Modoki' (Ilex serrata, var. Seiboldii), 'Momiji' (Japanese Maple), 'To-Kaede' (Trident Maple), etc., whose branches may wither because of the cold, should be taken into an unheated sunroom or be protected against frost. In this case, the protection against the cold should be barely sufficient to keep the soil in the container from freezing.

Showing how bonsai should placed. (Author's garden)

Unlike potted flowering plants, if a potted *bonsai* is placed in the ground, pot and all, the moss at the base of the trunk and the bark will be damaged.

Watering and fertilizer application.

Watering Clean rain water or city water should be kept in a tank built near the shelf for *bonsai* to keep it at practically the same temperature as that of the atmosphere. The reason is that if cold water is suddenly applied to a plant, the change in temperature causes its leaves to be damaged. However, there is no danger of such damage if the plant is accustomed to cold water from the time it started budding in spring.

There should be a watering-can with two roses, one with large holes and the other

Water should be kept in a tank so that it might be used soft.

Watering cans.

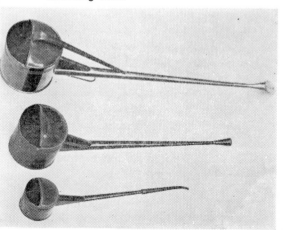

with fine. The roses should be changed to suit the occasion.

Two methods of watering are used. The first is to apply water only around the roots, and the second, to apply it so as to moisten the trunk, the branches and both sides of the leaves. The latter is called syringing. The former method should be used as often as the soil surface in the container becomes whitish and dry. When the edge of the container is much higher than the soil surface, water tends to accumulate in the container as a result of excessive water. On the contrary, if the container's edge is not sufficiently high, the water overflows too readily and causes water shortage. Plants whose roots are fully grown in the container absorb water more vigorously. 'Ume' (Flowering Japanese Apricot), 'Momiji' (Japanese Maple), 'To-kaede' (Trident Maple), etc., generally require abundant water, but the amount of water needed in each case also varies with the type of tree, the soil, and the manner of planting. Hence it is necessary to learn by experience the amount of water needed by each kind of tree as it is planted in the container. In general, it is sufficient to give water once or twice a day in spring and autumn, from two to three times a day in summer, and once every fourth or fifth day in winter. A sprinkler with small holes should be used when syringing or after transplanting while the soil has not yet settled. Otherwise, a rose with large holes should be used. Syringing means moistening the leaves, and this method is to be used after transplanting before the roots develop, and in summer when the temperature is hot and dry.

In the case of a newly transplanted tree, watering should be done once a day in fine weather. In the case of a plant with a fully developed root system, watering should be done in summer once a day early in the morning or in the evening, or twice a day, once in the morning and once in the evening.

In any case, it should be remembered that water is a very source of life to plants and without which plants can not sustain their life even for a single day. The need for water is all the greater in the case of *bonsai* which are plants planted in small containers

Syringing

with a limited amount of soil, and which have no other source of water-supply except rain, dew, and artificial watering. Thus, the absolute importance of watering should be fully recognized and practiced in *bonsai* growing. However, excessive watering jeopardizes the growth of branches and leaves, resulting in poor flowers and fruits. Under such circumstances, the tree is easily subject to attack by diseases and insects, and in extreme cases, the roots are even suffocated by the excessive water, causing the plant's death. Hence watering should be done in proper relationship to the state of dryness of the soil in the container as well as the color and growth of the leaves. In short, the fundamental principle in watering is not too much nor too little.

Fertilizer Fertilizer is to plants what food is to human beings. Fertilizer is absolutely necessary in the case of *bonsai* which are plants planted in soil containing only the minimum of fertilizer, and yet must develop a thick trunk, branches and leaves. *Bonsai* must also have all unnecessary branches pruned, and depending on the kind of tree, they must be made to bear flowers and fruits. The need for fertilizer is only too obvious. Without proper fertilizer application, proper plant growth can not be expected. Excessive fertilizer application naturally invites undesirable effects, causing root injury. The principal fertilizer for *bonsai*, esepcially for *bonsai* which is in the process of growing, should be rapeseed cake containing three elements—nitrogen, phosphate and potash in the proportion of 5:3:2 and the same should be applied in the safest and most effective way.

Three methods of fertilizer application

(1) Application in liquid form. 1.8 liters of rapeseed cake is diluted with three times the same amount of water, and the mixture should be allowed to decompose thoroughly. After the rapeseed cake has formed a sediment, the liquid at the top should be deluted with 5 to 15 times the same amount of water. This should be applied to the roots, but not to the base of the trunk itself. The liquid diluted with five times the same amount of water is considered strong, and that diluted with fifteen times the same amount of water is considered weak. The weak liquid fertilizer should be used from spring to summer, and the strong from summer to autumn.

This liquid obtained from rapeseed cake is ready for use after three weeks in midsummer, and after two months in winter.

(2) Application in powdered form. Rapeseed cake in powdered form may be put in

Three ways of giving fertilizer.

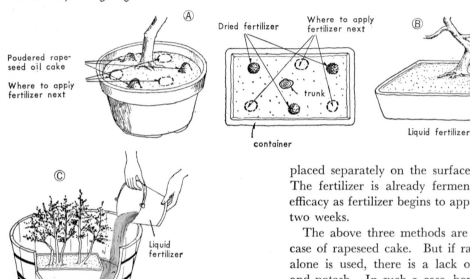

two or three lumps on the surface of the container soil. The amount of rapeseed cake in each lump should not exceed 1 to 2 spoonfuls, using a small teaspoon. This rapeseed cake gradually ferments and decomposes, and in about three to four weeks, begins to take effect as fertilizer. The lumps of rapeseed cake should be placed in different places the second time. This method is called "depositing fertilizer."

(3) Application in dried form. Rapeseed cake is kneaded with water, then it is made into round balls about two or three cm. in diameter. These balls are placed in a shaded airy place, so as to let them ferment, dry and harden naturally. The application method is similar to that used in the case of powdered fertilizer. Two or three balls are placed separately on the surface of the soil. The fertilizer is already fermented, so that efficacy as fertilizer begins to appear in about two weeks.

The above three methods are used in the case of rapeseed cake. But if rapeseed cake alone is used, there is a lack of phosphate and potash. In such a case, bone meal rich in phosphate content should be mixed. The ashes of plants rich in potash content, dissolved in water, may also be used in suitable quantities.

Application period Whatever the method, the period for fertilizer application should be from budding-time in early spring to about mid-July and from the end of August to the early part of September. The reason is that during these periods, the tree's growth is most vigorous. However, even during these periods, no fertilizer should be applied immediately after transplanting when the roots are not fully developed yet, and in the case of fruit-bearing trees, while the fruits are not quite ripe yet, especially during flowering time. Fertilizer application should be temporarily suspended during long rain and hot days in summer. This is to prevent root decay, and also because it jeopardizes respiratory action of the roots.

In the case of weak liquid fertilizer consisting of the decomposed liquid of rapeseed cake diluted with 15 times the same amount of water, application once a week is sufficient; in the case of strong liquid fertilizer diluted 5 times, once every two weeks, and for powdered and dried fertilizers, once a month. Sometimes, liquid, powdered and dried fertilizers are used together, appropriately decreasing the number of applications.

Besides the above, the following cautions should be observed in applying fertilizer:

(a) The number of applications should be adjusted in accordance with the growth of the buds, color of leaves, and the vitality of the tree.

(b) Fertilizer should not be applied when the soil in the container is dry. If it is dry, watering is necessary prior to fertilizer application. If fertilizer is applied to dry soil, the result is the same as if strong fertilizer had been applied.

(c) No fertilizer should be applied on rainy days, because it will be washed away and wasted. Fertilizer should be applied on fine or cloudy days.

(d) Early summer is the time the young leaves practically attain the full growth. Thus it is the time when the tree requires fertilizer most. So, many applications should be made during this season. The application in midsummer, when the temperature is high, only injures the roots. Fertilizer should be applied again only in autumn when the tree is ready to enter upon its period of rest.

(e) Trees whose purpose is the enjoyment of fruits should be given plenty of phosphate and little more than the ordinary amount of potassic fertilizer when they begin to bear fruits.

How to prune the buds.

When a tree planted in a container is taken care of according to the procedures explained on page 33, strong roots develop with simultaneous sprouting of new buds. In this case, the container should be left outdoors on a shelf to give it sufficient sunlight, besides plenty of water and fertilizer. This will stimulate the vigorous growth of new buds. At the same time, it will cause the sprouting of buds on the trunk and branches where there were no buds before. And sometimes, in the case of grafted trees, new buds will appear on the stock.

Why pruning is necessary If the new buds are allowed to develop freely, all the vitality of the tree will be concentrated on the tips of the buds which are in a favorable condition, while the other buds in the shade or are densely crowded will be subjected to an unfavorable condition, thus inviting poor growth. The former will grow into thick, long branches without any small ramifications, while the latter will become thin, weak branches. In both cases, the branches are either concentrated in certain parts and sparse in others, giving an unsightly appearance to the tree. To avoid this, as soon as the new buds begin to grow, proper bud-pinching should not be neglected, so as to remove buds from places where they are dense, leaving only the necessary buds which can be properly arranged into healthy branches.

The purpose of bud-pinching. Besides the above, there are other reasons why bud pinching is necessary.

(a) The pruning prevents the fresh buds from growing too long. It also helps the growth of underdeveloped buds. In the case of plants whose purpose is the enjoyment of their flowers or fruits, bud-pinching contributes to the better development of flower-buds.

(b) Bud-pinching helps the process of ramification. Especially in the case of autumn 'Momiji' (Japanese Maple) and other winter trees, whose purpose is the enjoyment of the appearance of the tree itself after the leaves have fallen, it is important to make the branches grow fine, tender and dense.

(c) Bud-pinching reduces useless consumption of nutrition. And it makes for more

Keyaki (Zelkova) whose shoots have been pinched several times to make the tips of the branches fine, soft and dense.

How to pinch shoots.

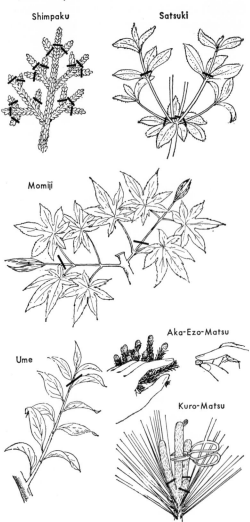

sunlight and better air circulation for the tree.

(d) The purpose of pinching is to improve the appearance of the tree, the development of the branches and leaves, and also the condition of fruit-bearing, by controlling the trunk and thick branches which constitute the main outline of the tree.

When and How to pinch the buds. Both the time and manner of bud-pinching vary with the kind of tree. Some varieties require bud-pinching only once, other varieties require it several times.

(a) 'Kuro-Matsu' (Japanese Black Pine), 'Goyo-Matsu' (Five-Needled Pine). With these trees, when the new buds have come out, but no leaves have developed yet, and the buds themselves are still soft, the longer buds should be pinched with a pair of shears, so as to leave a little portion of the base. If four or five buds have sprouted from one spot, cut off one or two from the base, then pinch the buds which have been left. Bud-pinching needs to be done only once.

(b) 'Aka-Ezo-Matsu' (Saghalien Spruce). When the eag-shaped buds (see illustration) begin to open their leaves, bud-pinching should be done once with one's fingernails.

However, as the buds are numerous, it is necessary to repeat the operation every day during the budding-season.

(c) 'Sugi' (Japanese Cedar), 'Tosho' (Needle Juniper). Whenever the buds at the tips begin to open their leaves, the tips of the buds should be pinched with one's fingernails. However, at those places where one wishes to start a new branch, the bud should be left un-pinched so that it will grow larger.

(d) 'Shimpaku' (Chinese Juniper). The center-buds at the tips should be pinched as often as new buds come out.

(e) 'Ume' (Flowering Japanese Apricot), 'Boke' (Japanese Quince), 'Kaido' (Showy Crab Apple), 'Sanzashi' (Chinese Hawthorn), 'Sakura' (Flowering Cherry), 'Tsubaki' (Camellia), 'Hime-Ringo' (Nagasaki Crab Apple), 'Karin' (Chinese Quince), 'Umemodoki' (Ilex Serrata var. Seiboldii). Unnecessary buds should be pinched from the base as soon as they come out. The buds that have been left should be allowed to grow. When the new leaves have all come out, the ends of those branches which have grown too long should be pinched once.

However, in the case of 'Umemodoki' (Ilex Serrata var. Seiboldii) which bears fruits on the young branches that have come out in the same year, it is necesary to leave a considerable number of flowers or fruits at bud-pinching time.

(f) 'Satsuki' (Satsuki Azalea). As several shoots will come out from the same bud, wait until all the shoots have come out, then keep one or two that show good growth and are properly located, and clip off the rest from the base. Then, the un-pinched shoots should be pinched leaving two or three leaves. Follow the same procedure for all the branches. Of course, where over many buds are crowded together, they should be pinched.

(g) Roses. Follow the same procedure as for 'Ume' (Flowering Japanese Apricot). However, do not pinch too deep. Pinching should be limited to the main buds at the end.

(h) 'Momiji' (Japanese Maple), 'To-kaede' (Trident Maple), 'Soro' (Loose Flower Hornbeam), 'Nire-Keyaki'. It is essential that these trees be grown in such a way that the ends of the branches will be fine, soft and dense. Hence, bud-pinching should be repeated from after budding-time in spring until the time of the reddening of the leaves in autumn.

(i) 'Kaki' (Japanese Persimmon), 'Kuri' (Japanese Chestnut). It is better not to prune the buds until the tree has borne fruits, provided that this does not cause the tree to loose its symmetrical shape too much.

Some Important Points to Bear In Mind When Bud-Pinching.

(a) No bud pinching should be done on trees that have been transplanted after trimming its roots or branches, until the trees have fully recovered their vigor.

(b) In the case of trees that require bud-pinching only once, the time of pinching is a most important factor. If the bud pinching is done too late, the secondary buds will not appear satisfactorily, with the result that the branches may be damaged by cold in winter. Again, if the bud-pinching is done too early, the buds will not grow large.

(c) In the case of 'Boke' (Japanese Quince), 'Satsuki' (Satsuki Azalea), roses, etc., which sprout buds promiscuously from the trunk, the branches, and even from the stock on which grafting has been done, it is important to clip off from the base, as soon as they appear, all buds that tend to grow into weak, long branches. If this pruning is done late after the bud has grown large, scars will be left. Such scars harm the dignity of *bonsai*.

(d) If pruning is repeated too frequently, it causes the withering of the branches. Therefore the vitality of the tree should be watched and one should see to it that bud-pruning is carried out properly at the proper time.

(e) Fresh buds which are soft may be pinched with the fingernails, but those which have hardened should be clipped off with the shears for bud-pinching.

Kinds of shears for pinching the shoots.

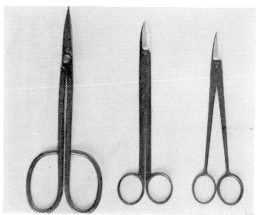

Control of injuries by insects and diseases.

Bonsai in containers as well as trees planted in the ground, are always subject to the attacks of insects and diseases which harm the proper growth of the tree, causing its appearance to be unsightly. In extreme cases, insects and diseases can cause premature falling of the leaves or fruits, withering of the leaves, or even the death of the tree itself.

Infestations of diseases and insects on one tree may spread. Particularly, insect outbreaks on one plant will spread to adjacent plants.

Although insects and diseases are vital enemies of *bonsai*, control thereof is a tiresome and tedious task to most beginners. Often no action is taken until the tree begins to wither. Then it is too late.

Therefore, careful watch should be kept on the outbreak of diseases and insects and if discovered, control measures should be carried out immediately.

Diseases of Bonsai

(a) Root-Decay. This is the disease that does the most damage. And there is hardly a variety of *bonsai* that is not subject to it. There are various causes. The soil may not have been mixed in the proper proportions, inviting poor water-drainage. Water might have accumulated at the bottom of the container. The soil in the container may be too dry. Transplanting may have been done at the wrong time. Too much water may have been applied after transplanting.

When a tree is attacked by this disease, its root system begins to decay, causing the leaves and branches to wither, and ultimately leading to the death of the plant itself.

(b) Nematodes. This causes wart-like swellings to develop at the trunk-base or on the roots. The tree loses its vitality and eventually dies. 'Boke' (Japanese Quince), 'Fuji' (Japanese Wisteria), 'Sakura' (Flowering Cherry), etc., are subject to it. It is contagious, depending on the type of soil.

(c) Mildew. This is the disease that causes the leaves and young branches of trees to appear as though they had been sprayed with flour. It is common especially in spring and autumn. 'Momiji' (Japanese Maple), 'To-Kaede' (Trident Maple), the roses, 'Kaki' (Japanese Persimmon), 'Hime-Ringo' (Nagasaki Crab Apple), 'Karin' (Chinese Quince) 'Umemodoki', (Ilex serrata, var. Seiboldii), etc., are particularly subject to it.

(d) Leaf spot. This is the disease that causes black, brown, or grey spots to appear in large numbers on the leaves. Sometimes these spots also appear on young twigs,

Control of the diseases stated above

Name of Disease	Means of Prevention	Means of Disease Control
Root-decay	Do not allow the above-listed conditions favoring the disease to prevail.	Replant as soon as possible. When replanting, cut off the dacayed roots and disinfect with mercury compounds.
Nematodes	When choosing a tree in the first place, choose one that is free from all diseases. New soil should be used each time.	When transplanting, cut off the wart-like swellings, immerse in lime, wash about 10 minutes, and then plant.
Mildew	See to it that the plant gets sufficient sunlight and air. All fallen leaves should be disposed of by burning.	Find a suitable preparation of an organic sulfur compound and spray it 2 or 3 times in the early stages of the disease.
Leaf spot	Gather up and burn all fallen leaves, fallen fruits and withered branches.	Spray with solutions of wettable or liquid preparation of Bordeaux mixture.
Rust	Gather up all fallen leaves and dispose of them by burning.	Find a suitable insecticide and spray for two or three days in the early stages of the disease.
Sooty mold	Exterminate all scales and aphids.	Spray with machine oil in winter. Spraying when the leaves are growing should be avoided as it soils the leaves and branches, besides causing troubles due to the insecticide used.

branches, and even on fruits. It appears most frequently in deciduous trees, especially in trees whose purpose is the enjoyment of their fruits.

(e) Rust. This is a disease which causes lumps of rust-like powder of yellow, orange, brown, reddish-brown, grey, white, etc., to grow on leaves and young shoots. It is very common in early summer. 'Sugi' (Japanese Cedar), 'Tsutsuji' (Azaleas), 'Satsuki' (Satsuki Azalea), the roses, 'Yusura-Ume' (Prunus tomentosa Thunb), 'Umemodoki' (Ilex serrata, var. Seiboldii), etc., are subject to this disease.

(f) Sooty mold. This is a disease which is caused by parasites such as scales, aphids, etc. The leaves and branches become unsightly as if they had been sprayed with soot. The tree loses its vitality perceptibly. The disease occurs most frequently in places where there is not enough sunlight or air. Broad-leaved evergreens are subject to this disease.

Insects that attack bonsai

Insects which damage *bonsai* in the United States differ from those found in Japan. However, in general, the following insects are the common enemies of *bonsai*:

(a) Insects that attack new shoots. The aphidaphid is an insect that attacks the new shoots of all kinds of trees and suck up their sap. The web-worm and the ume bud moth attack all varieties of the pine, 'Sugi' (Japanese Cedar), 'Ume' (Flowering Japanese Apricot), 'Sakura' (Flowering Cherry), the rose, the apple, etc. The insects eat their way into the new buds. The stem borers eat their way into the new shoots of pines.

(b) Insects that attack the leaves. The caterpillar and sawfly attack all varieties of the pine. The Japanese cedar tussock moth eats the leaves of 'Sugi' (Japanese Cedar) and 'Tosho' (Needle Juniper). The looper or canker-worm eats the leaves of 'Ume'

(Flowering Japanese Apricot), 'Boke' (Japanese Quince), the rose, 'Satsuki' (Satsuki Azalea), etc. Other injurious insects include the caterpillar, leaf roller, bag worm, etc.

(c) Insects that suck the sap from the leaves of trees. The red spider inflicts damage in hot, dry weather, sticking to the backs of the leaves of most trees. The lace bug sticks to the backs of the leaves of 'Kuro-Matsu' (Japanese Black Pine), 'Ezo-Matsu' (Saghalien Spruce), 'Satsuki' (Satsuki Azalea), 'Tsubaki' (Camellia), etc.

(d) Insects that attack buds and flowers. To this category belong the sawfly and the chafer.

(e) Insects that attack branches and trunks. The two most common types that belong to this category are the scales and the ruby scale. Besides these two are the 'wooly aphids which most commonly infect deciduous trees. The insects that dig tunnels in the wood part of trunks and large branches and cause the snapping or withering of branches are the borers.

(f) Insects that attack roots. The cutworm eats the roots of trees. Ants build nests in the roots of trees and injure their growth. Earthworm causes water leakage.

Control of the above insects

Since the United States has well developd in agricultural chemicals and control measures, the important thing is to find a suitable insecticide and use it effectively so as to prevent the spread of insects as quickly as possible. In controlling insects that injure *bonsai,* it should be borne in mind that, compared with trees on the ground, *bonsai* have less resistance to insecticides. And as *bonsai* are plants that give enjoyment even during their growth, when applying insecticides, care must be taken to avoid an excessive application. Care also should be taken to avoid such insecticides as remain a long time on the plant, harming its external appearance.

Protecting from cold in winter.

(1) Hardy *bonsai* which can withstand the cold easily, such as 'Kuro-Matsu' (Japanese Black Pine), 'Goyo-Matsu' (Five-Needled

Pine), 'Tosho' (Needle Juniper), 'Shimpaku' (Chinese Juniper), may be left on outdoor shelves even in winter. This is particularly true in warmer climates. However, when a *bonsai* is left outdoors, the container should be firmly tied to the shelf by means of string or wire to prevent its fall by the wind.

(2) Plants that need protection against cold. Even hardy plants which can withstand the cold easily should be protected against the cold when they have been recently transplanted and the roots have not yet fairly developed, or if there is danger of having their branches broken under the weight of the snow in cold districts.

All other varieties of trees, especially those that have little resistance to the cold because they are native to warmer climates, or plants like 'Keyaki' (Zelkova), 'Momiji' (Japanese Maple), 'To-Kaede' (Trident Maple), etc., whose branches wither easily in winter, or again, those that blossom early in spring, such as 'Ume' (Flowering Japanese Apricot), 'Boke' (Japanese Quince), should be placed where they will not be exposed to direct sunlight and be well protected against the cold.

Various methods of protection against cold.

(a) The simplest way of protecting *bonsai* against the cold is to put them under the eaves, near a window, or in a veranda, where they will be not subjected to wind, rain, frost or snow, and where it will be warm in

Examples of cold-proof installation for winter

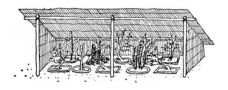

winter.

(b) Put the *bonsai* in a veranda, hallway, entrance, or sunroom where there will be plenty of light.

(c) Put the *bonsai* in a covered frame or a plastic house or a green house without any heating apparatus.

(d) Bury the pot in the ground where it is sunny and the water drainage is good. Build a simple protection over the *bonsai* against frost.

(e) Make a water-proof shelter by closing off with cloth the three sides facing north, east and west and the top. Leave the south side open to let in sunlight and place the *bonsai* therein. On very cold days, close the south side too with a translucent paper or plastic film screen.

(f) Around the *bonsai* shelf, build a shelter with waterproof cloth or jute sacks. Place the *bonsai* inside. On fine days, open the south side to let in air and sunlight.

(g) Dig a trench 60–100 cm. deep in the ground where the water-drainage is good. Build a sloping roof or a three-quarter roof over it about 30–90 cm. in height. The roof should slope toward the south. The three sides, north, east and west, should be closed off by means of boards. On the south side there should be windows with frosted glass to let in sunlight. *Bonsai* should be placed on the shelves built in this chamber. Steps may be made either on the east or west side for use as entrance and exit. (See illustration of cold-proof shelter in winter.)

How long to protect bonsai against the cold

Most *bonsai* should be placed in a cold-proof shelter after the frost season has set in, and the plant has been exposed once or twice to light frost. However, plants which are easily damaged by frost should be placed in the shelter before the frost season sets in.

In spring, bonsai should again be placed on outdoor shelves when the outer air has become warmer. This should be done before the new buds are still hard.

Principal points in cold-proof protection

(a) In putting *bonsai* in a cold-proof shelter, tall trees should be placed on the north side and smaller trees on the south, so as to provide the maximum sunlight to all plants. *Bonsai* of plants that require much light, such as 'Kuro-Matsu' (Japanese Black Pine), 'Goyo-Matsu' (Five-Needled Pine), 'Ezo-Matsu' (Saghalien Spruce), 'Tosho' (Needle Juniper), 'Shimpaku' (Chinese Juniper), 'Ume' (Flowering Japanese Apricot), 'Boke' (Japanese Quince), 'Kaido' (Showy Crab Apple), 'Sakura' (Flowering Cherry), 'Keyaki' (Zelkova), etc., should be placed where plenty of light is available, while plants which do not require so much light in winter, such as 'Sugi' (Japanese Cedar), 'To-Kaede' (Trident Maple), 'Momiji' (Japanese Maple), the ivy, 'Umemodoki' (Ilex Serrata, var. Seiboldii), 'San zashi' (Chinese Hawthorn), 'Hime-Ringo' (Nagasaki Crab Apple), 'Satsuki' (Satsuki Azalea), etc., should be placed where there is less light.

Recently transplanted plants with undeveloped root systems or plants whose trunks or branches have been cut in order to arrange the shape of the tree, should be placed at the furthermost end in semi-shade.

(b)   Providing heat by means of fire in the cold-proof shelter is not necessary. It is sufficient if the temperature is kept so that the soil in the container will not freeze. Therefore, *bonsai* should not be brought into a heated room. If it must be put in such a room, it must be only for a short period of time, a week or so. If a *bonsai* is kept in a heated room, watering should not be neglected to prevent soil drying. If the plant is kept in such a room too long, instead of resting, it will put forth buds. This weakens the plant when the time for proper activity comes.

(c)   Water should be given each time the soil surface in the container becomes dry and white. Water should be poured on until it begins to flow out of the hole at the bottom of the container. From time to time, water

Example of a shelter for *Bonsai* in winter.

should be syringed on the leaves of the plant. This syringing of water on the leaves of *bonsai* is necessary, as *bonsai* are not exposed to the dew at night. Giving water on the leaves is particularly effective in the case of 'Kuro-Matsu' (Japanese Black Pine), 'Goyo-Matsu' (Five-Needled Pine), 'Ezo-Matsu' (Saghalien Spruce), 'Shimpaku' (Chinese Juniper), 'Iosho' (Needle Juniper), 'Ume' (Flowering Japanese Apricot), 'Boke' (Japanese Quince), 'Keyaki' (Zelkova Tree), so that it should be repeated every other day or so.

(d) Letting in fresh air is something that tends to be neglected most easily with *bonsai* in the cold-proof shelter. Even in winter, the temperature goes up quite high during the daytime. The humidity is very great as a result of evaporation. This excessive moisture is harmful to the plants. Therefore, during the daytime, the cover of the shelter should be removed to let in fresh air.

(e) Most trees rest during the winter season when they are placed in a shelter. So no fertilizer is needed. But even in winter, harmful insects, such as aphids, red spiders, scales, etc., continue their destructive activities. Therefore disinfection against such insects should be done once or twice even while the tree is in a period of rest.

(f) The container should be rotated from time to time to ensure that every part of the tree gets the same amount of light on an average. This is necessary to make the plant bud evenly in spring. This is a precaution which should be observed not only in dealing with plants placed in a cold-proof shelter, but with plants placed outdoors. Again, if the containers are kept in the same position all the time, some will get enough water, but others will not.

(g) In spring, if the plant is suddenly taken out of the cold-proof shelter into the open and placed in an outdoor shelf, the abrupt change in temperature can be injurious. So, before taking the plant out, the heavy covering for protecting the plant against frost should be removed in fine weather, several days before the plant is to be taken out. The plant should be accustomed to the outside air gradually. These plants which bud first should be taken out first.

If a *bonsai* is properly taken care of during the period of winter rest, it will develop into a fine tree in less than a year. Trimming the branches and improving the general appearance of the tree is the next step; but the efforts so far will have already given the beginner some idea of the pleasure of growing *bonsai* and stimulate him to even further efforts in future.

INTRODUCTION TO BRANCH ARRANGEMENT

Need of arranging the branches.

Bonsai is an art that primarily values nature. However, as *bonsai* are plants planted in a small amount of soil in small containers, they cannot be expected to grow freely with long, thick branches and luxuriant foliage, the same as natural and wild trees in the mountains and forests.

Accordingly, if a tree is grown for several years in a container, its development is hampered and the tree becomes compact. However, mere smallness of size does not make a *bonsai*. The reason is as explained in the opening paragraphs of this book that merely the small size of a plant does not constitute the primary purpose of *bonsai,* which is the reproduction in miniature of the appearance of a huge old tree or a bit of natural landscape.

For the growing of *bonsai,* certain special techniques for caring are vitally required, besides fertilizer application and bud pinching as stated above. This special care consists chiefly of arranging the trunk and branches and is a labor which no *bonsai* grower can afford to neglect.

The aim of branch-arranging.

The purpose of branch-arranging is to correct and improve the shape of a plant by removing unnecessary branches. It also aims to straighten unsightly bends or to collect or separate branches taking care to enhance the natural characteristic of the tree. At the same time, branch-arranging aims to create a gracefulness of form, most befitting the tree, and to increase its value as a *bonsai.* Excessive bending or twisting of branches should be avoided.

Technique and know-how are needed for branch arranging.

Arranging the branches of a *bonsai* is no easy task. In fact, it is one of the most difficult techniques involved in the art of *bonsai* growing. Accordingly, to ensure complete branch arranging, one must visualize the ultimate shape of the tree and should be equipped with know-how to carry out the branch arrangement without hurting the tree.

This sounds baffling to a beginner. However, with the aid of a guide-book, and also by studying the methods of more experienced persons, one can start with the easier methods, and gradually master the whole art. The important thing is to make patient efforts to achieve the know-how and to acquire the needed skills.

Once the technique of branch arranging is acquired, it is easy enough to arrange the branches of any *bonsai,* regardless of kind. Interest, too, will increase proportionately.

Various ways of arranging the branches.

Generally speaking, the following three methods are used in branch-arranging. Each of these methods is based on the appearance of large, old natural trees and the graceful shape of trees as depicted in Chinese paintings.

Arranging with a pair of shears This is the method which consists of using a pair of shears to cut off unnecessary buds and branches in order to arrange the branches.

Supporter

Example of arranging by suspending the branches.

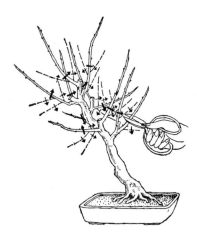

Example of arranging by pruning with a pair of shears. Arrow shows where the cut is to be made. The dotted line shows where the young twigs will appear next.

It is enough if one has two kinds of shears, one for pruning the branches and the other for pinching the buds. However, with shears alone, it is not possible to perform such major operations as bending or straightening thick branches. Large scars left on the tree are very unsightly. The tips of the branches can become rugged.

Suspending the branches This method consists in arranging the branches by pulling the branches sideways or obliquely downwards by means of strong but soft twine or wire. Sometimes a piece of wood is applied to the branch.

This method is satisfactory in the case of trees that are soft and easily breakable, or in the case of trees whose bark is soft and easily scarred. Such trees are 'Sugi' (Japanese Cedar), 'Momiji' (Japanese Maple), 'To-Kaede' (Trident Maple), 'Keyaki' (Zelkova, 'Umemodoki" (Ilex Sarrata, var. Seiboldii), etc. This is also the method used by people who have no confidence in arranging by wiring to arrange the branches. However, it is by no means the best or the safest method in all cases.

The two preceding methods were the methods used until about 1890 when the art of growing *bonsai* was not so highly developed. However, since the discovery of the epoch-making method of arranging by wiring, neither of these methods is much used.

Arranging by wiring This method consists in tying wire around the trunk or branches and bending or straightening them in the direction or angle desired. This is the most advanced and most effective way of branch-arrangement. The only drawback is that it is a method which requires knowledge, skill and proper tools. However, once the technique is mastered, it can be used for a lifetime. Therefore, this method of arranging by wiring will be explained in this book because it is the method most generally used at present.

Tools and materials needed for arranging by wiring.

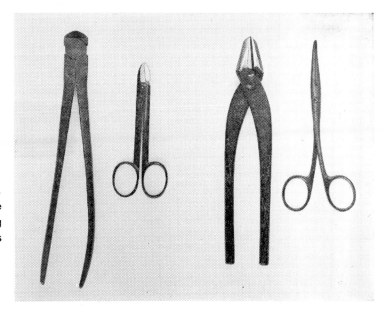

Left to right: Root cutter, nail-clipper for cutting fine wire, pincers for bending thick wire, and light pincers for thin wire.

Tools A pair of shears for cutting wood, another pair for making deep cuts, a small-sized saw, a knife, a pair of pincers, a pair of pliers, a lever for arranging the branches, a revolving table, etc. A jack may be necessary for bending at an acute angle the trunk or a thick branch of a tree that is particularly hard in quality. The lever for arranging branches is used when dealing with branches that cannot be safely handled by hand. The other tools are those in ordinary use.

Materials

(a) Wire. This is the most important. There are many varieties, such as iron wire, zinc-coated iron wire, steel wire, but none of these are suitable, because all those wires are hard and difficult to handle. Moreover, they rust easily, absorb heat, and harm the bark, or spring back to the original position.

In comparison with the said types of wire, copper wire is softer and can be bent or stretched with ease. Being soft, it does not injure the bark. Nor is there any danger that copper wire will spring back to the original position. Copper wires will stay in place for years. Moreover, the same wire can be used repeatedly. It is the most suitable. However, it is the most expensive in price. It develops poisonous verdigris when it rusts.

If one has only one kind of copper wire, one cannot vary the thickness with the purpose one has in mind. Hence, one should generally keep about seven or eight kinds of different thickness, varying from 5.16 mm. to 0.56 mm. With the 5.16 mm. wire, it is possible to bend trunks whose circumference is about 6 cm. With the 0.56 mm. wire, the thin, fine twigs of 'Shimpaku' (Chinese Juniper), 'Keyaki' (Zelkova), etc., may be bent or stretched.

However, of these various kinds of copper wire, the most commonly used is the medium type, ranging from 2.76 mm. to 1.65 mm. Ordinarily, a piece of wire is used alone, but sometimes, two or three wires are wound together for greater strength to take the place of thicker wire.

Copper wire has the property of hardening as soon as it comes in contact with moisture. Hence, when using copper wire, straw or hay should be burned to make a weak fire. This rids the wire of moisture and softens it.

The copper wire which has become soft should be wound onto a spool for greater convenience in later use. When storing copper wire, a dry place should be selected.

In using used copper wire, the same procedure should be followed. That is, it should be heated with a weak fire so that all the twists will be taken out, and then wound onto a spool. If such wire is used, it will absorb moisture again and stay in place like any other wire.

(b) Paper tape. Copper wire is a good conductor of heat. Hence, when it is used for arranging branches, it can be heated to as high as 100 degrees Farenheit in summer, and cause the trunk or branches to be burned. This is particularly true in the case with 'Sugi' (Japanese Cedar), 'Momiji' (Japanese Maple), 'To-Kaede' (Trident Maple), 'Keyaki' (Zelkova), etc., which have a tender bark, or with the young twigs of other trees.

Again, if copper wire is used to arrange branches by bending them at a very sharp

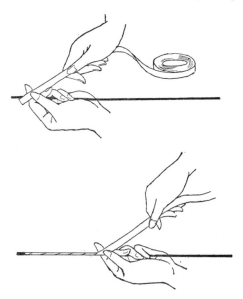

How to wrap paper-tape around copper wire.

angle, the wire cuts into the branch, inflicting damage. Sometimes, it can even cause the branch to break or to wither.

Hence, in cases where such danger is expected, paper-tape should be wrapped around the copper wire before it is used. This will also prevent the generation of poisonous verdigris from rusting.

(c) Raffia. No raffia need be used when arranging young twigs by wiring, but it is necessary in the case of trees whose quality is easily breakable, or in the case of trees with a soft bark that is easily scarred, such

Three ways of wrapping raffia. Arrow shows the direction in which tree is to be bent.

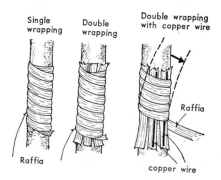

as 'Nishiki-Matsu' (a variety of Japanese Black Pine), 'Momiji' (Japanese Maple), 'To-Kaede' (Trident Maple), etc. It is also necessary when arranging the trunk or thick branches of a tree, or when dealing with trees whose bark might be scraped off, such as 'Goyo-Matsu' (Five-Needled Pine).

The purpose of the raffia is to protect the place where the wire is to be applied. It should be applied horizontally, or both horizontally and vertically, to the trunk or branch that has to be bent. The wire is applied over the raffia. If just one wrapping of raffia is not sufficient, then one to three pieces of thick copper wire should be placed inside the branch to be bent, and then wrapped with a double layer of raffia arranged both horizontally and vertically.

(d) Covering. When applying wire to a tree with a soft bark, or when bending with a lever an old trunk or thick branch of a hard quality, the use of some covering as a protection is necessary. In these cases, the

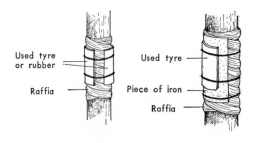

How to use coverings.

mere use of raffia is not enough. Some covering should be used where a sharp bend is desired or where a lever is to be applied to lighten the pressure.

Used tires, rubber hose, or sheet iron may be used as covering. These materials should be cut into suitable sizes and wrapped with raffia.

(e) Adhesive Plaster or Wax Cloth for Grafting. Adhesive plaster or wax cloth may be applied to places where cuts have been made in the trunk or in a thick branch to prevent decay and also hasten the healing process.

The foregoing is a brief explanation of the use of the tools and materials used in arranging the branches. However, in the case of a beginner who is trying to make a *bonsai* from a young tree, a cutting, or a grafted tree, all he needs are two or three varieties of copper wire of medium thickness, some paper tape, raffia, and a pair of shears for cutting wood.

Time for arranging by wiring.

The time for arranging by wiring varies with the kind of tree and climate. In applying the technique to young twigs, that is, twigs that sprouted in the spring of the same year, the proper time is when the twig growth has slowed down to some extent as the leaves achieve maturity. The same is true for branches and trunks two to five years old.

The reason is that the circulation of the sap is very active and the branches and trunks are resilient, which makes it easier to work on them. When a branch is bent in a desired direction during this time, there is little danger that it will be hurt. As time goes by, the tree will assume the desired shape.

However, in the case of 'Kuro-Matsu' (Japanese Black Pine), 'Goyo-Matsu' (Five-Needled Pine), etc., which are trees the cir-culation of whose sap begins in early spring, arranging by wiring should be done a little earlier.

On the contrary, in the case of trunks and thick branches that are several years old, arranging by wiring should be done some-time between the commencement of the cir-culation of the sap in spring and the time when buds begin to develop. It is true that around this time, the branches and trunks are easily breakable and the vitality of the tree is at a low ebb. It is not the best time for the operation. However, this is the time when *bonsai*-growers have a comparative degree of leisure. Hence, major operations can be performed without endangering the new buds. If sufficient care is exercised after the operation, there is no harm in choosing this time.

Preparation for arranging by wiring.

The tree whose branches are to be arranged by wiring should be given sufficient fertilizer from the previous year. If sufficient fertilizer is applied, a tree naturally tends to grow soft, which facilitates work and lessens the chances of injury to the plant. The tree will be able to withstand much more strain than ordinary.

Do not give too much water. If a tree is watered too much prior to arranging its branches by wiring, hardness sets in and the trunk and branches become difficult to bend.

Accordingly, watering should be avoided for a day or two prior to the wiring. The soil in the container should be dry.

All the necessary tools should be on hand. Especially the cutting tools should be very sharp. Otherwise, the results will not be satisfactory.

The operation should be performed in-doors where there is plenty of light. There should be no direct sunlight, nor any wind or rain. A chair and a rather low table are needed, so that the work can be done seated. A revolving table is very handy. The *bonsai* is then placed on the revolving table for the operation.

The front and back of bonsai. Tcshō (Needle Juniper)

(Front)

(Back)

Determining the front and back of the *Bonsai*.

There are some *bonsai* which are beautiful from any side or angle. However, such trees are very rare, and most trees are beautiful only when viewed from one side. The side that presents the most pleasing view, either because of the vitality of the roots or the manner of their growth, the condition of the trunk, whether straight or bent, the condition of the bark, the foliage, etc., should be chosen as the front side of the *bonsai*. The opposite side, then, is the back. The terminal of the tree at the very top should be slightly inclined forward. This is the proper position for all *bonsai*. The viewing of a *bonsai*, should be done from the front.

There are many unwritten laws concerning *bonsai*. Hence it is necessary, even when arranging the branches of a tree, to determine at first which side shall be the front and which the back. In order to determine the front side of a *bonsai*, one should place it on a table, so that the middle of the tree will be about as high as one's eyes. The tree should then be turned and examined closely to find which side is the most beautiful. When a tree is to be planted in a container, the same procedure should be followed, so that the front of the container and the front of the plant will match. In this way, both the plant and the container can be viewed from the side that looks best.

Determining the shape of the tree.

The shape of a *bonsai* varies with each tree. In fact, there are no two trees of an identical shape. This adds much to the charm of *bonsai*.

There are certain general types which can be classified as follows:
1. "Chokkan" (straight trunk) A single tree with a straight trunk.
2. "Sha-kan" (slanting trunk) A single tree with a slanting trunk.
3. "Ban-kan" (twisting trunk) A single tree with a twisting or gnarled trunk.
4. "Ryu-boku" (single tree) A single tree which cannot be classified under any of the above three preceding categories.
5. "Kengai" (cascade tree) A single tree whose trunk hangs down in one direction.
6. "Han-Kengai" (semi-cascade tree) A single tree with a leaning trunk and thick branches that hang down in one direction.
7. "So-kan" (twin trunks) A tree whose trunk is divided into two trunks near the roots, so that two trunks, one thick, the other thin, grow up in parallel line.
8. "Kabu-dachi" (grouped trees) A tree divided into several trunks near the roots, so as to present an appearance of a group of trees.

9. "Yose-ue" (combination of trees) Several trees planted together.
10. "Ishi-zuke" or "Ishi-zuki" (trees planted on a rock) A tree or trees planted on a rock or rocks.

There are merits and deamerits to each of the forms above. The important thing is to determine at the outset which of these forms is to be adapted for one's *bonsai*. This decision should be made upon close examination of the overall appearance of the tree as viewed from the front.

In making this decision, such factors as root growth, tree growth from the ground, together with the size and condition of the trunk and branches, the harmony between the branches and the trunk, etc., should be kept in mind. And then try to visualize the tree-form most suitable to the tree. When a general form is visualized, all unnecessary branches should be cut off, and where branches or trunks are missing, wires should be used to pull them into the required places, thus giving the tree the desired shape. If a beginner wishes to give the tree a new form, the safest way is to try to bend the trunk in the direction opposite to the branch.

Unnecessary branches must be cut off.

Before wiring the branches of a tree, all unnecessary branches should be cut off, both to improve the shape of the tree and also to make work easier.

Unnecessary branches are defined to mean: (1) Branches which have grown too dense, (2) Withered branches; (3) Branches which have grown inward; (4) Comparatively thick branches that have grown toward the front of the tree.

How to cut off the branches.

Young trees. The manner of cutting off the branches varies with each tree, but in the case of young trees whose branches are to be arranged by wiring for the first time, attention must be paid to the following points.

If the lowest branch to be left is on the right side, the next branch to be left must be on the left side, and the third branch should be on the right. At the top, one thin terminal should be left. All other branches should be cut off from the base as they are unnecessary. The first branch, the second branch and the third branch are the important branches. If the lowest branch is on the left side, the second branch should be on the right. In other words, the important branches should alternate, and there should be one thin terminal at the top.

Thus the general shape of the tree is determined by the three branches and the terminal at the top.

Older trees. The same procedure can be applied to wild trees uprooted from forest or mountain and transplanted into containers with well developed branches and foliage on which wiring can be made. In this case there may be more than just three branches to leave. In fact, four or even five branches may be left, in alternate order, the first one on the left, the next one on the right, etc. Other unnecessary branches should be cut off. For the top, one branch as close to the top of the tree as possible should be left. The places where thick branches have been cut off should be smoothed and covered either by adhesive plaster or by wax cloth. **Trees in the process of growing.** In the case of a tree whose branches are being arranged by wiring, it is only necessary to cut off the withered branches and those of the new branches which are unnecessary, as the main branches and the top should have

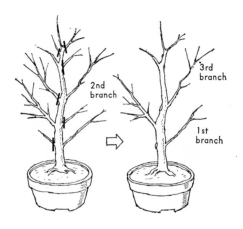

How to thin out the branches of a young tree.

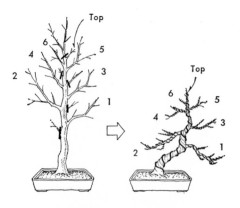

Showing how the branches are arranged by bending the trunk sharply at the main branches.

Example showing how the branches of an old tree obtained from the mountains are arranged.

Example showing how the branches of a tree obtained by layering are arranged.

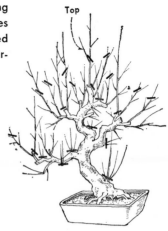

already been matured. In doing this wirings of the previous year still on the tree should be removed, beginning with the thinner wires near the edges and gradually proceeding to the thicker wires.

In this case, the old wire is hard, especially the thicker type, and there may be some that have cut into the bark. These should be cut by means of pincers, so that the bark may not be hurt in the process of removing the wire.

Order of wiring

Before going into a detailed explanation on wiring the order of wiring procedure should

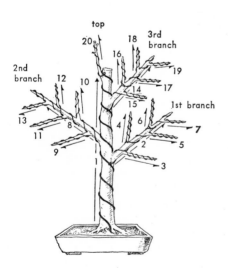

Showing the steps of wiring the branches. The wires should be applied in the order of the numbers and in the direction indicated by the arrow.

be mentioned first.

In the case of young trees, (1) start at the bottom and gradually move upwards, (2) after wiring the trunk, start with the base of the first branch and proceed toward the tip; (3) then begin the wiring to the first twig on the first branch, and proceed toward the end, then proceed to the next twig on the same branch; (4) when wiring has been completed on all the twigs on the first branch, then proceed in the same manner with the twigs on the second branch; (5) then proceed to the third branch. Lastly, begin at the bottom of the terminal and proceed to the tip.

In the case of older trees. This manner of wiring is satisfactory with young trees, but in the case of older trees, there will be more branches naturally, so that wiring becomes considerably more complicated. Therefore, in the case of such a tree, begin where it is easiest for wiring. Those branches which are more difficult may be left to the last, and if some branch is unusually difficult to be wired, then just leave it.

If a straight trunk is desired, the slightest bend or twist in the trunk should be corrected. Trees with twisting trunks which may be interesting should be corrected to fit one's taste. Sometimes it is far more interesting to have a certain curvature in the trunk.

The above are some example of wiring a tree. Particularly, in the case of young trees which have not developed any special characteristics, it may be necessary to wire the whole tree to give it a desired shape. This, of course, is no easy task. But it is a delightful task which gives the *bonsai*-grower infinite joy.

Since the wiring method varies considerably with the age of a tree, wiring in both cases will be described.

Wiring of a young trunk. First place the container on a table. Then, bearing in mind the shape which you wish to give the tree, apply both hands to the part of the tree that requires either bending or straightening, beginning with the lower part, and softly bend the trunk several times. After this, making sure that the trunk can be bent as far as you wish, proceed with the wiring.

How to bend the trunk with hands.

The copper wires tied to the trunk should be thick enough to prevent it from springing back to the original position. If the trunk is the thickness of one's thumb, the thick-

ness of the wire should be in proper proportion thereto. The wire may be applied directly to trees with a hard bark, like pines, but in the case of trees with a soft bark, like 'Momiji' (Japanese Maple), 'To-Kaede' (Trident Maple), 'Keyaki' (Zelkova), 'Umemodoki' (Ilex Serrata, var. Seiboldii), 'Sugi' (Japanese Cedar), etc., the wire should be wrapped with paper tape.

In the case of 'Satsuki' (Satsuki Azalea) whose bark is so soft that the wire cuts into it even if it is wrapped with paper tape, raffia should be wound around the places of wiring.

One end of the wire should be firmly fastened before wiring the trunk. This fastening is very important, for if the wire is not properly fastened it will have no effect. The best way is to bury one end of the wire to reach the bottom of the container. As the inside of the container is filled with the root system, the wire can not be pulled out so easily.

Showing how paper-wrapped wire is thrust in to the bottom of the container along the trunk.

However, if the wiring place is far above the base of the trunk, covering should be used first. Then the trunk is wired by fastening it. And if this is not possible the wire should be tied to one of the main branches for fastening.

After the wire is fastened, it should be cut at a suitable length about 9 to 15 cm. longer than the entire length of the trunk. This excess length is necessary to allow for winding the wire; and the more winding there is to be done, the longer is the excess length of the wire.

If the wire is closely wound spirally, it will not hold. And more wire is needed.

Arranging the branches of Toshō (Needle Juniper) which was wired last year.

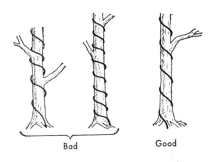

Bad   Good

Technique of applying the wires. In bending, apply constant pressure with the thumb

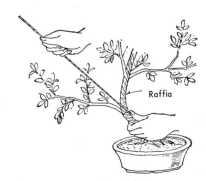

Raffia

How to wrap wire

The wire should be wound slowly with one hand with sufficient spaces between the rings. As the wire is wound, use the thumb of the other hand to press it against the bark. It should be neither too loose nor too tight. While winding the wire, the hand should never be released. If it is released, some parts of the wire will be wound tightly and other parts will be wound loosely, with the result that the wire will not hold at all.

At places where the trunk is to be bent or straightened sharply, the wire should be wound in such a way that it will be wound on the outside. This will make the wire hold better.

 Wrap wire so that it will come on the outside of the place to be bent sharply.

When winding the wire, care should be taken not to break the branches.

After the wire has been wound, its end should be bent with a pair of pliers, and then cut with a pair of pincers, after making sure that the wire will not spring back to its original position.

After the wire is wound, the trunk is ready for bending or straightening. In this process too, one should begin at the bottom, near the roots.

Grasp with both hands a little above and below the place that is to be bent, press the thumbs against the trunk, and bend it to the desired position. When doing this, be sure to bend the trunk in the direction of the wire, twisting it slightly with the wire. This will make the wire take better effect. In the case of trees that snap easily, it is enough merely to bend the trunk. When the twists have been straightened, the work of applying wires to the tree is completed.

Wiring of a tree 6—7 or even 10 years old.

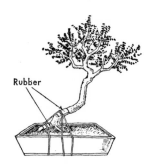

Fasten the base of the trunk so that the tree will not move.

First make sure that the trunk will not move by fastening it to the container with twine. Then place the container on the table, and begin to work on the tree according to the preconceived image of the plant. Begin always with the lower part of the trunk.

Quite unlike the young trees described above, there are trees whose trunks are so thick and hard that bending with the hand is difficult. Before wiring such trees, use a pair of pruning shears or a lever for branch-arranging in order to make bending easier.

How to cut the trunk by the root-cutter.

The pruning shears are a convenient tool to use when a trunk has to be bent at an acute angle to give the tree the desired shape. If one or two cuts are made vertically at the place where the trunk is to be bent, the bending can be done with ease. However, these cuts inflict a wound on the trunk. So the use of this method is not suitable for trees in which such injuries are slow to heal. It may be used for 'Kuro-Matsu' (Japanese Black Pine), 'Aka-Ezo-Matsu' (Saghalien Spruce) etc., whose wounds heal quickly.

The lever for arranging branches has three advantages: It does not injure the trunks or thick branches of trees; it is suitable for bending and straightening branches; and it is simple and durably built. The instrument has been devised by the author himself based upon his experience of several years, and designed especially for the use of *bonsai*-growers.

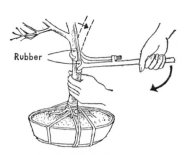

Technique of bending the trunk with a lever.

As shown in the illustration, first apply a piece of rubber or a tyre a little above or below the place that is to be bent. Then lock the lever. Next, apply a similar covering to the inside of the place to be bent.

Apply the end of the lever and gently pull the handle and bend the trunk to the desired position. Repeat this two or three times until the trunk can be bent with ease. Then remove the lever.

When straightening a trunk that is bent, the process is practically the same. Use two levers, one a little above and the other a little below the place to be straightened, pull the handle gently upward at the same time, and stop when the trunk has become straight. Repeat the process two or three times until the trunk can be bent easily, then remove the levers.

After making the trunk easily bendable by this means, wire should be applied, using, in the case of trees with easily damaged bark,

raffia which is wrapped in one or more layers. The wire itself should be covered with paper tape.

The manner of winding the wires is similar to the manner used in the case of young trees. However, when using two or three thin wires instead of one thick wire, care should be taken so that the wires do not become entangled. They should be wound so that they will lie side by side in parall lines and adhere closely to the bark.

After the wires have been wound, the lever should be applied again in the same manner as before. The trunk is bent to the desired position together with the wire. Lastly the lever is removed.

How to apply wire to branches.

Branches that grow upwards have more vitality. They lose this vitality when they are pulled down to a horizontal position or lower. The former type of branches are found on young trees, while the latter type are found on old trees. This is something that all *bonsai*-growers must remember.

In wiring the branches, one should start with the first branch. Use wire which is thinner than that one used for the trunk.

However, it should be sufficiently thick so that it will not spring back. In the case of trees that snap easily or those whose bark is easily injured, raffia should be wound around the branches, and paper tape should be wrapped around the wires.

The manner of applying the wire varies, depending on whether the tree is young or old, whether the branches are thick or thin, etc. In general, however, the wiring of

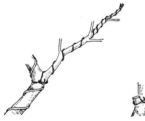 

How to secure the wire to be applied to a branch.

thick branches is the same as the wiring of the trunk. Now, the wiring of a thin branch and a young twig will be explained.

How to wire the branches of a young tree. Fasten the wire first by tying it to the trunk or tie it to the wiring on the trunk. If there is a part of a withered branch near the first branch, the wire may be fastened to that. In any case, the wire should be so fastened that it will not move.

The wire which has been fastened should

be cut at a length which is from 3 to 9cm. in excess of the length of the branch.

The wire should be wound, starting with the base and working toward the end. It should be so wound that it will stick closely to the bark. Care should be taken not to break any of the small twigs in the process. The end of the wire should be wound twice and fastened tight so that it will not spring back. Cut off the excess wire with a pair of pincers.

Sometimes a branch may be forked into two smaller branches. This can happen to the trunk, too. In such a case, if the wiring is below the two branches and if it is done separately above the two branches, the result is unsightly and moreover, the wiring does not work. Therefore, make sure that the

How to apply wire to forked branches.

wire is long enough for both branches. Wire the middle of the fork and fasten. Then wind the wire clockwise on one branch and counter-clockwise on the other.

After the wire has been attached, the main branch should be bent, starting at the base. This bending should be done with various factors in mind, such as the total appearance of the tree, the condition of the growth of the smaller branches, etc. The balance of the upper part with the lower, the left with the right, the larger branches with the smaller, etc., should be considered so that the branches will have the appearance of the lower branches of an old tree.

This can be done with both hands in the case of young trees and trees that are about ten years old, without special instruments. The only thing to be remembered is that when bending a branch, strength should be applied not only to the finger-tips but to the thumbs as well.

After wiring the first main branch, the next step is to wire the small branches at the base of the main branch, moving gradually toward the end. The following three points should be borne in mind while performing this operation:
1. The wire used should be thinner than in the case of the main branch. One end of it should pass through the wire attached to the main branch, and its end should be bent with

Set up the tips of the small branches to prevent weakening.

a pair of pliers so that it will stay in place.
2. After winding the wires on all the small branches of a larger branch, one should see to it that the small branches do not overlap. The small branches should be spread out evenly so that every branch will receive the same amount of sunlight.
3. The ends of the small branches should not be pulled down. This causes decline in the vitality of the tree and may even cause the branches to wither. Hence the very tips should be raised somewhat.

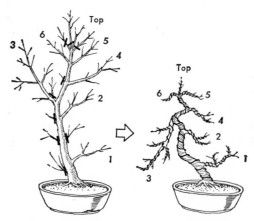

Comparing the appearance of the tree before and after arranging its branches by wiring.

The same procedure should be followed with the second and third branches, proceeding gradually toward the top of the tree.

The main branch should be pulled downward as far as the third or the fourth branch. However, in the case of the main branch, the pulling should not be below the second or the fourth branch. The branches above it should be directed horizontally or upward, so that the tree will take on a natural form.

Sometimes, it is desirable to shape a branch at a certain place that seems somewhat bare. With such a tree, choose a branch nearby and change its direction, or pull a branch into position and thereby arrange the desired shape.

In this case, if a branch is to be bent to the right, the wire should be wound to the right, and if it is to be bent to the left, it should be wound to the left. The reason for this is that in a case like this where the branch is to be bent at a sharp angle, the branch is bent in the direction in which the wire is wound, and not only the branch, but the wire with it, otherwise the wire will be ineffective. Danger of damaging the branch will be invited unless this precaution is taken.

In this operation, the branch to be bent should be covered with raffia. The wires should be wrapped with paper tape, also. The operation should be performed in such a way that the artificial treatment will not be perceptive.

How to apply wire to a new shoot.

The proper time for wiring new shoots is when the leaves on the twig have more or less matured and the twig itself has grown fully so that its growth is no longer perceptible, and hardening has set in in the lower parts.

When wiring is carried out at this time, the new shoots have sufficient resiliency, so that not only is the wiring process made easier, but there is less danger of damaging the tree. The wiring retards the growth of the new twigs, so that excessive development is checked in the case of young twigs that have too much vitality. Moreover, the wires which have been applied begin to take effect as the new twigs harden. So effective are these wires that after two or three months, the branches are properly arranged.

Hence the wiring of young shoots has the effect, not only of checking undue growth, but also of giving the tree the desired shape.

In wiring the branches, dense and unnecessary shoots must first be cut off from the base. Of the new shoots that are left, only those should be arranged by means of wires that give indication of improper development.

As the bark of new shoots is soft, and there is danger that the wire will cut into it, paper tape should be wrapped around the wire. No special tools are needed. The twig is bent two or three times to the angle or position desired. And after the twig has become accustomed to being bent, fasten one end of a piece of wire and wind the other end to the twig, starting at the base.

How to apply wire to a new twig.

The same technique can be applied to the main branch. But care should be taken not to tear off the leaves in the process.

After the wire has been wound around the twig, bend the twig to the desired position, and then pinch the tips of the buds on the new twigs. However, if the branch is bent down altogether, it loses its vitality. Raise the very tips to prevent this.

Wiring the terminal.

After the wiring has been completed on all the branches, the terminal should be pointed upward. If the single terminal at the top of the tree is raised, the vitality of the tree will be concentrated there, and the result will be that the *bonsai* will grow too tall. Moreover, it can cause the lower branches to wither. Handling becomes difficult, too. Accordingly,

Top

New top

How to make a
new top.

with most *bonsai,* the trunk is cut at about

the middle, and the terminal of a branch is raised instead.

In the case of a tree in the growing stage where it has no terminal as yet, or because even if it has a terminal, its position is too high and unsightly, a new terminal must be created. To create a new terminal, choose a small branch with good leaves near the tip of the tree, and cut off all branches above it.

Wire the branch which is to be made into the terminal. The wiring should be done from below so that the terminal will stand up straight. The very tip of the terminal should be inclined somewhat toward the front.

Caution to be taken in wiring.

1. Remember that wiring a tree is irritating

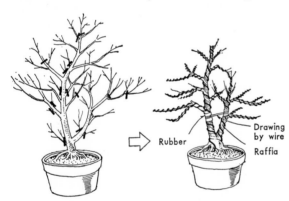

Rubber

Drawing
by wire

Raffia

Example of a tree whose branches have been arranged by combining the two methods of arranging by wiring and suspending the branches.

to the plant. Thus, every step should be taken carefully.

2. In winding wire, do it in a single operation without repeating.

3. In bending a branch after the wire has been wound, it should be done somewhat twisting the branch in the direction in which the wire is wound, and never in the opposite direction.

4. If wiring a tree is not enough to arrange its branches, use the technique called suspending the branches. In this case, when the branch is to be suspended at an acute angle, apply raffia and also pieces of rubber where there will be contact with the wire.

5. Begin wiring a trees which is easy to handle. After having mastered the technique, proceed to more difficult trees.

Wiring and the height of *Bonsai.*

When the wiring of a tree is completed, the trunk and branches will be bent, and as a natural consequence, the *bonsai* tends to be smaller in height. Of course, the small height depends on the degree of the curvature of the trunk and branches. Small height is one characteristic, and the fact is in itself a welcome feature of *bonsai.* What is the proper height of a *bonsai?* This again depends on the grower, his taste, the place where the

bonsai is grown, the amount of help available, etc., but from the point of view of care and enjoyment, the proper height should be from 45 to 55 cm. Those larger than this size are called large-sized *bonsai,* and those which are smaller are called small-sized *bonsai.*

Those whose height does not exceed 12 cm. are called miniature *bonsai.* However, such extra-small *bonsai* are very difficult to take

Large, small, and miniature *bonsai*.

proper care of, nor can they give the true delight that real *bonsai* offer.

How to treat *Bonsai* after they have been arranged by wiring.

After wiring, it must be remembered that the tree is considerably exhausted, so that it must be given a rest. For this, the container is placed where there is no wind and no direct sunlight. Give it plenty of water, pouring it on the entire plant. Do this once or twice a day for some time after the wiring. When the plant has completely recovered its strength, put it back on its outdoor shelf.

The period of rest to be given to *bonsai* depends on the extent of wiring. Ordinarily three to four days is considered a suitable rest. A tree which has been subjected to a major operation needs a rest-period of about a week. During this period, neither fertilizer nor insecticide should be applied. After the *bonsai* has ben restored to its outdoor shelf, fertilizer can be applied again.

How long does it take for a branch to bend after it has ben arranged by wiring? With proper wiring, younng twigs and thin branches bend in about two to three months. Thicker branches take from three to four months. With some, one has to wait more than a year before the branch bends.

If the wires do not produce the desired results, what should be done? For instance, if the wires should cut into the bark, they should be removed at once. If the wire has produced no result, either the method was wrong, or the tree is one that does not bend easily. Simply try again the following year.

Arranging the branches by wiring is no doubt a difficult technique, but if one does it himself, he is sure to enjoy the pleasure of *bonsai*-growing, even if not always successful.

SOME POINTS TO BEAR IN MIND IN TAKING CARE OF *BONSAI*

Bonsai should be watched with constant affection.

Bonsai is the art of planting a tree in a container, and growing it as a healthy plant by giving it infinite care so as to be able to enjoy a miniature replica of graceful natural scenery. So it is important to watch over one's *bonsai* with unfailing affection. Any person who wishes to grow *bonsai* should, at least, spare ten to twenty minutes every day, either in the morning or in the evening. Without such effort, successful *bonsai* growing can hardly be expected.

And if one has a true affection for his *bonsai,* he cannot fail to take notice of the drying of the soil in the container, the condition of the buds, the color of the leaves and the growth of the new shoots which determines the amount of fertilizer to be given, the infestation of insects or disease, the condition of the flowers and fruits, the withering of the leaves, the decay of the roots, etc. And upon finding such defects, some countermeasure must be taken.

It is impossible to overestimate how important it is for the *bonsai* to be watered when the soil becomes dry, or to have insects controlled. The very first step in *bonsai* management is to watch over one's plants daily with genuine affection, and if anything is wrong, then some countermeasure must be taken immediately.

Transplanting

Purpose The purpose of transplanting is to change the soil in the container before the container becomes filled with the plant's root system, preventing the soil from functioning properly as well as to give the new roots a chance to develop fully.

When to transplant The time a plant requires to fill the container with its roots varies with the type of tree, its vitality, growing stage, fertilizer management, soil mixture, etc.

However, in general, a tree in the growing stage should be transplanted once a year, while a full-grown tree, once every two or three years. Pines are exceptions and need transplanting only once every four or five years. As for other types of trees, the time for transplanting is shown in the chart at the end of the book.

Transplanting soil and method The subjects of soil composition and the transplanting method have been already discussed in the Introduction to *Bonsai* Growing (page 24).

In transplanting, the old soil should be removed as thoroughly as possible, and the ends of the fine roots pruned. All unnecessary branches should also be cut off to improve the appearance of the tree. Then plant the tree firmly in the container with good water drainage.

The container for transplanting In transplanting a tree with a definite shape, a container should be selectd whose shape and color harmonize with the tree. This is to enjoy the container as well as the plant.

Some examples of containers suitable for certain types of plants are as follows:

For evergreen, needle-leafed trees, use containers of red earthenware, dark grey earthenware, violet earthenware, or containers of imported Chinese earthenware.

For evergreen flowering trees, use grey-

Aka-Ezo-Matsu, (Saghalien Spruce) being transplanted from a pot for growing into a *Bonsai* container

colored containers.

For deciduous flowering trees, use celadon porcelain containers if the flowers are white or yellow, and use grey ones if the flowers are red.

For deciduous trees with autumn tinted leaves, use celadon porcelain, or grey or white earthenware.

For deciduous trees with fruits, use white earthenware, white cochin-china, or violet earthenware.

Where to put *Bonsai* and the question of fertilizer application.

This subject has already been discussed in the section on trees for practising. The important thing to remember is that, after transplanting, a plant has to be treated with extra care until the roots develop. When the roots have developed, the plant may be placed on an outdoor shelf, but it must be given plenty of water so that it will not become dry. Weak fertilizer should be given several times whenever the plant needs it.

A tree in the growing stage should be given proper care so that it will take on a pleasing shape. For such a tree avoid the hastening of bearing of flowers or fruits, but concentrate on growing a healthy tree. Apply sufficient fertilizer during the growing season. Give the trunk and branches a chance to grow thick and let the tree assume more or less a definite shape. In the case of flower-or fruit-bearing trees, apply phosphatic or potassic fertilizer in considerably large quantities to stimulate blossoming and fruit-bearing. The ideal way of fertilizer application is one which ensures the enjoyment of flowers and fruits for a long time.

Pinching the buds and arranging by wiring.

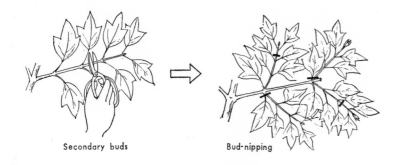

Secondary buds   Bud-nipping

How to prune the shoots of *To-Kaede* (Trident Maple), Momiji (Japanese Maple), etc. In the case of trees whose shoots appear in opposite, prune the shoots alternately.

As a tree grows, new buds tend to sprout more and more. So the densely grown buds should be pinched as soon as possible. Buds which have appeared on opposite sides should be so pinched as to leave alternate buds. Every care should be given to ensure the healthy development of the buds that have been left after pinching.

Pinching the buds To ensure the growth of fine and dense branches at the tips, pinching should be repeated so as to increase the number of sprouting buds.

However, in the case of trees with flowers on new twigs or those with a danger of the branches withering in winter as a result of pinching, the time for pinching should be postponed until after the new shoots have grown long and have begun to swell or to become hard. Then the tips of the more energetic new shoots should be pinched.

There are some cases in which the new shoots grow too vigorously, with the result that the internodes become too large, or the shape of the tree becomes unsightly because of the new shoots standing up. Such trees should be arranged by wiring which will retard the growth and by pulling down the branches to give a proper shape. These wires must be removed in autumn before they cut into the bark.

Control of insects and diseases

The infestation of insects and diseases is common with *bonsai*. Under such conditions as lack of sunlight or air circulation, plant nutrition shortage, poor plant growth is inevitable. Accordingly, control measures should be taken in the first place by spraying regularly in winter or in spring just before the buds come out, at budding time in spring, or in dry hot weather in early summer when the outbreak occurs frequently.

If an outbreak occurs, the infected part should either be cut off before spreading of the infestation and be burnt, and the insects should be caught and killed or an effective insecticide should be applied.

Cutting the leaves.

The technique is to arrange the tree shape by growing soft, delicate and dense branches. 'Momiji' (Japanese Maple), 'To-Kaede' (Trident Maple), 'Keyaki' (Zelkova), 'Nire-Keyaki' (Chinese Elm), belong to this class of trees.

Method of cutting The method is to cut the leaves with a pair of specially made light shears about two months after transplanting when the leaves on the new twigs have sufficiently developed. The leaves should be cut, starting at the top of the tree and work-

Weak branch

Healthy branch

How to cut the leaves of Momiji (Japanese Maple).

ing gradually down.

However, the way of cutting the leaves varies with the type of tree and branch. For instance, in the case of 'Momiji' (Japanese Maple) or 'To-Kaede' (Trident Maple), all leaves are cut from about the middle of the leaf stalk, but if an important branch is in a weakened condition, the leaves on that particular branch may be left uncut, or even if the leaves have to be cut, only the tips of the leaves are cut off and the remaining half of the leaves are left uncut.

In the case of 'Keyaki' (Zelkova) or 'Nire-Keyaki' (Chinese Elm), the leaves are far smaller and more numerous than in the case of the maple, so that cutting every leaf is a tedious task. With such trees, all unnecessary tips should first be cut off with a pair of shears, and then the remaining leaves should be cut off with a pair of shears or with the fingers.

Do not cut the leaves of a weakened tree Leaf-cutting is a drastic operation for a tree, so that it should be avoided in the case of weakened trees. Again, before the leaves of any tree are cut, plenty of fertilizer should be applied beforehand in order to strengthen the tree. This is a precautionary measure to ensure safety.

After the leaves are cut, the tree should be watered well and then it should be put on an outdoor shelf to give it enough sunlight. Watering should be done two to three times a day to induce the sprouting of the buds. If this is too troublesome, the plant should be kept indoors in a place with plenty of light. Water should be sprinkled on it once a day until the buds begin to appear. It can be taken outside after that.

When the buds have begun to appear, the plant should be sprinkled every day. Liquid fertilizer might be applied from time to time so that the tree might recover its strength all the sooner. With the measures stated above, the growth of smaller and denser leave can be ensured, and the tree will come to have branches of a delicate and graceful appearance.

Momiji (Japanese Maple) ten days after its leaves have been cut.

Various protective measures.

Cold proof measures and control of insects and diseases have been discussed on page 39 and page 41 respectively. So the counter-measures for the damage caused by the wind and domestic animals, such as cats or dogs, will be discussed.

Considerable damage is done by the wind. This is particularly true of *bonsai* that are placed on a high table or shelf. Still, it is not desirable to place the containers directly on the ground because that will cause both the container and the leaves to be soiled by mud. Earthworms might also creep into the container through the hole at the bottom and inflict damage. Moreover, containers on the ground are hard to take proper care of. If the containers are placed on stones, bricks, tile or concrete, the roots suffer from the cold in winter, while in summer, the strong heat can also do harm to the plant.

Accordingly, shelves or tables made of thick boards are the best. When placing the container on a shelf, it is wise to tie it securely to the shelf so as to prevent its fall when a strong wind blows.

Damage from domestic animals Domestic animals are a nuisance to *bonsai*. Because of the habit of dogs and cats always to urinate at the same place, *bonsai* should never be placed on the ground.

Carving in order to conceal a scar.

Bonsai should be void of any scars. If a plant has a conspicuous scar its value as a *bonsai* will be greatly reduced. So when the trunk is damaged by insects or diseases or is decayed or scarred or when a branch shows a conspicuous scar, carving is done in order

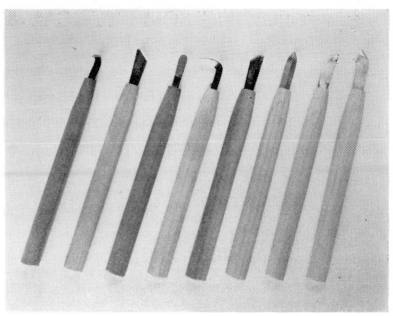

Various kinds of knives for carving the trunks or branches.

to conceal all such unsightly spots.

How carving is done Carving should be done indoors during the plant's winter rest-period. The base of the trunk should be tied firmly to the container so that the plant will not move. Use a sharp carving knife and gradually carve out the decayed or withered part. Of course, care should be taken not to hurt any of the living part of the tree or its leaves.

Carve out the decayed part in such a way that the hole made in the tree will resemble the natural hollow found in most old trees. Leave the hard core, and smooth the surface of the part that has been carved. Then apply adhesive plaster or wax cloth to prevent further decay.

A *bonsai* on which carving has been done should be taken care of in a warm room, and for some time, it should be watered every day to stimulate the recovering of its vitality, and also to promote the healing of the wound. Some weak fertilizer might be used for the purpose.

If the plant is taken care of in this manner, the part around the wound will begin to develop in due time. After two or three years, the scar will hardly be visible.

Some *bonsai* with grace and dignity, which have *shari-kan* or weathered dead branch or trunk, are made in this way.

Tosho (Needle Juniper) with " *Jin* " (dead and weathered top)

67

GROWING SOME TYPICAL *BONSAI*

———————Needle-Leafed Evergreens.———————

Kuro-Matsu (Japanese Black Pine)

Characteristics This is a very hardy type of tree, and will survive hundreds of years

Kuro-Matsu (Japanese Black Pine)

even in a container. The trunk becomes thick, the bark rough, and the branches vigorous. Its evergreen leaves pointing toward the sky certainly is a masculine feature. The shape of the tree increases in elegant grandeur with the age of the tree, and its beauty is indescribable. It is a tree most suitable for growing as *bonsai*. Its growing is easy, too. As it is a tree that can be viewed with pleasure all the year round, it is considered as belonging to a class superior to other types of trees.

Material Tree The best tree for this purpose is an old dwarfed tree that might be uprooted from a rocky mountain about the time the new buds begin to appear. The leaves of such a tree are small, dense, and beautiful. Those which have hard barks with cracks are more highly valued. Prune the large roots to conveniently suit the container. Then prune the branches and leave the soil attached to the root system as much as possible. Plant the tree in the garden and leave it there for a year or two, applying large amounts of fertilizer to develop its fine roots. Dig out the plant again in spring just before the buds come out, and plant it firmly in an unglazed pot, using soil containing 20 to 30% coarse sand to facilitate water drainage.

Growing Place the container in a place where there is plenty of sunlight and air all the year round. Salty breezes do no harm, but dust and the exhaust gas of automobiles are harmful. Water the tree as often as the surface of the soil in the container becomes dry. In very hot weather in summer, syringe the leaves. For fertilizer, use only rapeseed cake. After the roots are fully developed, deposit two or three table spoonfuls of powdered or dried fertilizer about three times a year. A white myceloid membrane which forms at the bottom of the container is an indication that the pine is growing vigorously.

Pinching The buds should be pinched rather closely, varying, however, with the length of the new shoots. After about a month or so, two to three secondary shoots begin to appear from the base of the shoots that have been pinched. As these secondary shoots cannot grow too long, both the branches and the leaves become smaller, which is desirable in the case of a *bonsai*.

Removing old leaves and insect control. The leaves of 'Kuro-Matsu' (Japanese Black Pine) generally last for two years, but when they grow old, they become dusty and unsightly. Hence, the old leaves should be torn off after the lingering heat of summer is over. Again, while a tree is in the growing stage, infestation of red spiders, caterpillars and wooly aphids is common. This should be controlled by insecticides.

Arranging the branches by wiring The best time for this is in spring before the buds come out. The wires may be used without any wrapping. But if there is any fear that the bark will come off from the trunk or from a thick branch that is to be bent at an acute angle, raffia may be wrapped around the place which is to be bent.

Carving Scars made by cutting the trunk or a thick branch should be carved indoors during the winter to make them look as natural as possible. In the case of withered branches, peel off the bark and then remove the soft wood part, so that the result will be a '*jin*' (or weathered dead top). Such a *bonsai* will have a beauty all its own.

Transplanting At first, the tree should be transplanted every three years, but after the initial period, transplanting should be done once every four or five years. The proper time is when the new buds come out. As for the soil, it should be red clay and coarse sand mixed in the proportion of 7–3 respectively.

Other trees that may be treated in the same way as 'Kuro-Matsu' (Japanese Black Pine). There are various varieties of 'Kuro-Matsu' (Japanese Black Pine), varying with the place of growth. 'Nishiki-Matsu' whose bark is very rough so that it shows cracks like the back of a turtle, is one variety. 'Aka-Matsu' (Japanese Red Pine) is an entirely different species, though it resembles 'Kuro-Matsu' (Japanese Black Pine). Its bark is finer and smoother and has a reddish color. Its leaves are finer and softer and the shape of the tree is characteristically feminine.

Both of these trees can be grown as *bonsai* in the same way as 'Kuro-Matsu' (Japanese Black Pine). In the case of 'Nishiki-Matsu', however, one should start with a grafted tree or a cutting.

Nishiki-Matsu (Japanese Black Pine) with extraordinarily developed cork-tissue.

Goyo-Matsu (Five-Needled Pine)

Characteristics It is a hardy tree that, like 'Kuro-Matsu' (Japanese Black Pine), will live for hundreds of years in a container. The growth is slow, but the trunk becomes thick and the branches numerous. The bark resembles that of 'Akamatsu' (Japanese Red Pine) but is finer. The leaves are short, grow in clusters of five, are evergreen and have a white line in them. The shape of the tree is graceful and feminine. As the tree grows older, its dignity increases. It is a beautiful tree that lends itself particularly to growing as a *bonsai* because of the various shapes that it can be made to take. It has the additional advantage of maintaining its shape for several years, once it has been given a certain shape. Together with 'Kuro-Matsu' (Japanese Black Pine), it is counted among the best trees for growing as *bonsai*.

Kinds and Strains There are different kinds and strains depending on where the tree grows. Some have a bark that is thick and coarse, others a bark that is thin and fine. Some varieties have long, thick and curving needles, while others have short, thin and straight ones. There are different colors for the needles, too, such as silver, gold, dark and pale. Besides these different strains, there are some that grow on high mountains, whose trunks crawl on the ground, and are for that reason called 'Hai-Matsu' (Dwarf Stone Pine).

Of these numerous kinds, the one best suited for growing as *bonsai* is the kind with short, small, and dense leaves, delicate ramifications whose internodes between branches are not too long, and whose bark is thick and rough. Particularly, the kind called dwarf 'Yatsu-Busa-Shō Goyo-Matsu' (Five-Needled Pine with Eight Clusters) has short dense leaves and branches. It is dwarfed in nature and is much prized by *bonsai*-growers. This type is ideal for growing as a miniature *bonsai*.

Material for the Art of Bonsai In the case of 'Yatsu-Busa-Shō Goyo-Matsu' (Five-Needled Pine), it is best to begin with a cutting or a grafted tree. In the case of the other kinds of 'Goyo-Matsu' (Five-Needled Pine), use an old tree that has been dwarfed

Goyo-Matsu (Five-Needled Pine), with layering applied.

in the high mountains, or a natural seedling. Trees grown by grafting or layering may also be used. However, if a grafted tree is used, care should be taken to choose a tree in which the joint is perfectly healed, otherwise one cannot grow a good *bonsai* from it. In the case of obtaining a tree by layering, remember that it takes two to three years before the roots develop.

Fertilizer application Fertilizer application is the same as in the case of 'Kuro-Matsu' (Japanese Black Pine). The only difference is that more fertilizer is needed. Hence, after the roots have developed after transplanting—in those years when the tree has not been transplanted, after the new buds have begun to grow—deposit two or three teaspoonfuls of fertilizer on the soil in the container about 5 or 6 times a year.

Pinching and removing old leaves This, too, is to be done as in the case of 'Kuro-Matsu' (Japanese Black Pine). However, as the new buds of 'Goyo-Matsu (Five-Needled Pine) are shorter, only the tips of the buds should be pinched. Old leaves of a yellowish color should be removed by hand, taking care not to injure the bark.

Pruning the branches All unnecessary branches should be pruned when the old leaves are removed, or in spring, before the buds come out. This arranges the shape of the tree. Of course, the places where the branches have been pruned should be made smooth, and when the wound is large, measures should be taken to prevent decay.

Arranging by wiring and carving When the sap is flowing vigorously, the branches are resilient, but the least wound causes the secretion of resin, which interferes with growth. Accordingly, in the case of 'Goyo-Matsu' (Five-Needled Pine), arranging by wiring should be done in winter. Bare wires are used. However, in bending the trunk or a thick branch, plenty of raffia should be used. The wires must be changed every two years.

If carving is necessary on the trunk or branches, it should be done immediately be-fore the wiring. After the wiring, the tree should be allowed a rest period so that it may recover its vitality.

Transplanting Transplanting should be done in the warm spring. If the tree is transplanted too often, the leaves tend to grow too long. Hence, it should be done once in four or five years. Of course, when root-decay has set in or when the branches have begun to wither, it is necessary to transplant immediately, regardless of when it was transplanted last. The soil for planting should be red clay and coarse sand, mixed in the proportion of 7–3 respectively.

Control of injurious insects Red spiders, aphids, wooly aphids, and scales are common insects. Insecticides should be kept on hand ready for spraying upon need.

Aka-Ezo-Matsu (Saghalien Spruce)

Characteristics Since this tree has only a short history as *bonsai*, it is not known how long it will live in a container. However, it is a very hardy plant which resists cold, snow, dryness and poor soil. Seeing how if flourishes in a container, developing fine branches and leaves, it is safe to assume that its life-span is at least as long as that of 'Kuro-Matsu' (Japanese Black Pine) or 'Goyō-Matsu' (Five-Needled Pine).

This is a plant which is indigenous to cold climates. Accordingly, its growth is slow, but its bark is rough and has an elegance all its own. Its leaves, as compared with those of 'Goyō-Matsu (Five-Needled Pine), are much smaller and denser, and they do not fall for several years. The beauty of its buds in spring is remarkable. It is suitable for growing as a *bonsai,* as it can be made to take almost any desired shape. And once the tree has been givn a certain shape, it retains that shape for several years. Like 'Goyō-Matsu' (Five-Needled Pine), this tree increases its value as *bonsai* with more care.

Kinds and Varieties The so-called 'Ezo-Matsu' (Saghalien Spruce), is correctly called by *Bonsai* growers 'Aka-Ezo-Matsu' and has rounder leaves which are thick and short, dense and yellowish-green in color.

Aka-Ezo-Matsu (Saghalien Spruce). " San-kan " (Three trunks style)

The buds are particularly beautiful. The trunk is yellowish-brown. The growth is very slow. But the ordinary 'Ezo-Matsu' or 'Kuro-Ezo-Matsu' (Yesso Spruce), on the contrary, has flat leaves, which are somewhat long and narrow and dark green in color. They are not so dense, nor are the buds so beautiful to to look at, therefore it is rarely grown as *bonsai*. The trunk is greyish-black in color and grows rather quickly.

For purposes of *bonsai*, the Saghalien Spruce is more suitable. Sometimes, we find a variety of Saghalien Spruce called the Eight-Cluster Saghalien Spruce. The leaves of this variety are particularly short and dense, and the branches ramify into numerous smaller branches. It is a beautiful plant of a dwarfed form. It does not take long to grow it from a sapling as *bonsai*. It is particularly siuted for growing as a miniature *bonsai*, and is now considered the king of the Yesso Spruce family.

Material Tree The best tree is an old tree which has survived the harshness of nature among the tundras of the arctic region for 200 to 300 years. The plant is uprooted and planted firmly in a container with good water-drainage, filled with red clay and coarse sand mixed in the proportion of 8-2 respectively. The container is then placed in a place where there is no wind and where the sunlight is weak. The leaves of the tree should be syringed frequently to help the roots to develop.

If a suitable material plant can be found, choose a part where the branches are shapely, and in the season when the buds come out, peel off the bark round the branch to a width of about 3 cm. at the place where one intends to root the branch. Then smear some red clay mixed with water onto the place from which the bark has been peeled. Apply some wet sphagnum moss in a lump above the cut. Cover the moss with thin polyethilene film and fasten it by means of some thread. See to it that the moss does not become dry. After the roots have developed sufficiently, the tree should be cut from the mother plant. If this method called layering is used, one can easily obtain a tree in half a year from a mother plant that is 9 cm. in diameter.

Cuttings of shoots are easily made to grow too. Saghalien Spruce and Eight-Cluster Saghalien Spruce may be used for cutting off small branches that are from two to three years old, in the warm spring. These branches should be about 9 to 15 cm. in length. They should be planted either in flat boxes or shallow pots, just like any other cutting. Frequent watering of the leaves expedites growth. Within half a year, a tree is grown which can be used as a tree for practicing the art of *bonsai*.

Giving Fertilizer The place for putting the container is the same as far 'Kuro-Matsu' (Japanese Black Pine). In mid-summer, however, the container should be placed where it is cool. The plant should be given sunlight all the year round. Between the time of planting and the growing of roots, both the roots and the leaves should be watered sufficiently for about a month. Otherwise, the plant should be watered at the roots until summer, and that in small quantities. This is to prevent the leaves from growing weak.

From early summer and all through the summer season, water should be given to both the roots and the leaves in order to prevent leaf-scorching and branch-withering. Care should be taken not to let the branches, leaves and trunk get too dry. As for the rest, ordinary watering should be sufficient.

Fertilizer application is the same as in the case of "Goyō-Matsu' (Five Needled Pine). But in the case of a young tree, growth will be stimulated if fish manure is mixed with rapeseed cake.

Pinching The shoots which are to grow long must be left unpinched, but those which have appeared in undesirable places to have the branches or the leaves to become dense must be pinched, beginning with those that begin to grow long first. The length of time for pinching to be done varies with the age of the tree and also the number of the small branches, but in the case of a tree whose shape is more or less definitely made, about two weeks should be enough, provided pinching is done every two or three days.

Arranging the branches by wiring Arranging by wiring should be done when the leaves have become hard in the case of new twigs, and in the case of branches and trunks, during the winter season. Bare wires may be used. But when bending old branches or trunks at an acute angle, raffia should be wrapped around the places to be bent. So long as there are no twists in the wires, they need not be removed, but in general they should be removed every two or three years and replaced by new wires. Those branches on which other unnecessary branches have grown should be cut off at the time the wires are applied.

Control of injurious insects Borers attacking new buds, and red spiders that infect the tips of new buds are the two great enemies. To eradicate the same, BHC should be sprayed for the former and TEPP for the latter, just before the new buds come out.

Transplanting Transplanting should be done once in two years in the case of trees in the growing stage and in the case of trees with permanent shapes, once in every four to five years. The proper time is in spring when the buds begin to come out. The soil is the same as for 'Goyō-Matsu' (Five-Needled Pine). Young trees should have their roots pruned rather close, while older trees should have them pruned less closely, before they are transplanted firmly with good water drainage.

Carving The same process should be used as for 'Gōyo-Matsu' (Five-Needled Pine).

Sugi (Japanese Cedar)

Characteristics This is a hardy, rapid-growing tree. It is adapted for growing in a container in which it survives a long time. The trunk is strong and straight, and the tree is particularly remarkable for the way it rises out of the ground. The branches ramify into numerous small branches, and the leaves are dwarfed in nature and dense. Though an evergreen, the tree changes the color of its leaves with the changes of the seasons. It is suited for growing as *bonsai*, especially as a *bonsai* of "Chokkan" style which has a single straight trunk. A tree which has been carefully grown in a container has the appearance of an old tree towering in the mist in the deep mountains. Such a tree also reminds one of a solitary tree that stands in a field, presenting a noble spectacle. It has a salient beauty of its own.

Varieties There are numerous varieties of 'Sugi' (Japanese Cedar). Of these, the one best suited for purposes of growing as a *bonsai* is 'Ma-Sugi' (True Japanese Cedar). But of this 'Ma-Sugi' there are various kinds again, differing in bark, leaves, etc. Accordingly, care should be given in choosing one with small leaves that grow dense, and a thick coarse bark.

Material tree If one is fortunate enough to find a tree in the mountains with good leaves and bark, roots firmly developed, branches spread, and a trunk growing straight out of the ground, uproot it in spring just before budding-time. In this case, if the trunk is too thick, the tree tends to be too tall. Moreover, it will be no easy matter to cut the trunk properly. So, the diameter of the trunk should not exceed 3 to 6 cm. and the height should not be over 45 to 61 cm. Anything beyond this should be cut off. The cut part should be made smooth and pointed.

'Sugi' (Japanese Cedar) can easily be obtained by layering. Hence, trees may be used that have been obtained by layering, in the same manner as in the case of 'Aka Ezo-Matsu' (Saghalien Spruce).

The above measures are applicable in making an average-sized *bonsai*, but if a small-sized *bonsai* is desired, a seedling or a cutting is generally used. The former is slow in growth, so that it will take at least 7 to 8 years before the tree has taken on a definite shape. The latter is quicker in growth, so that in 4 or 5 years the plant is ready for viewing as *bonsai*. However, in point of value as *bonsai*, the latter is no match for the former.

Fertilizer application The tree must be planted firmly, but not too deep, in a container with good water drainage. To ensure the same, use coarse sand at the bottom. The container must be placed in a place where there is both air and sunlight. In summer, however, the container must not be left in the direct sun, and in the afternoon and in winter, it should be placed indoors in a place where there is plenty of light. Otherwise, it should be put in a cold-proof shelter to protect it against frost.

Watering should be done so that the soil in the container is always somewhat wet. Give plenty of water in summer once in the morning and once in the evening. Weak liquid fertilizer consisting of the decomposed liquid of rapeseed cake should be applied, about twice a month during the growing season. If during this time, the weakened decomposed liquid of dried squid is given from time to time, the color of the leaves will be greatly improved.

Pinching The finer and denser the tips of the leaves, the more beautiful does 'Sugi' (Japanese Cedar) look. Thus, during the growing season when the buds grow, pinching should be repeated several times. The use of shears is highly undesirable for this purpose. Although the work is tedious, the pinching should be carried out with the fingers. When the new buds of bag-like shape have attained a length of about 15 mm., the tips should be pinched, so that the leaves will swell and become round.

Adjusting the Branches and Arranging by Wiring In early spring, just before budding time, all withered branches and dense branches should be cut off. Over-grown branches should be pruned to arrange the tree shape. At the same time, unsightly branches and branches that interfere with proper tree shape should be arranged in place by wiring. However, in the case of

Sugi (Japanese Ceder)

growing a "Chokkan" style or a *bonsai* which has a single straight-trunk, wiring should be no more than a mere aid.

Transplanting A tree that is still in the process of growing should be transplanted once in every two years. All other types of trees should be transplanted once in every three or four years, during early spring. The soil should be a mixture of 5 parts of black loam, 3 of coarse sand, and 2 of leaf mold.

Carving and the Top In the case of 'Sugi' uprooted from the mountains, if its tip or a part that has been smoothed and made into a point is carved in winter to make a white bone-like "jin" (weathered dead top), the *bonsai* will have increased dignity. One should not forget at this time to attach wires to a good branch in the neighborhood in order to raise the next growth point.

Deciduous Flowering Trees

Ume (Flowering Japanese Apricot)

Characteristics This is a particularly hardy, rapid-growing tree. It withstands the cold very well, and bears beautiful flowers long before all other trees in early spring. It has a refreshing fragrance, too. The trunk shows a variety of curvatures, and the bark is very

Shidare-Ume (Flowering Japanese Apricot with droopping branches)

Ume (Flowering Quince) Miniature Bonsai.

strong and coarse. The manner in which it stretches its branches has an air of primitive grace. The tree increases in dignity as it grows older. Its shape as wel as its flowers offers perpetual enjoyment to all who view the plant. It is suitable for purposes of *bonsai,* as it can be made to take almost any shape. Moreover, it is easy to grow, has a long life-span, and with good care, its value as *bonsai* can be greatly increased. When in bloom, the tree is indeed the king of *bonsai.*

Varieties At one time, there were more than

300 varieties. But at present, the number has been reduced to about half, out of which only about one-third or about 50 varieties are suitable for *bonsai.* These 50 varieties are roughly classified into two groups according to color, white and red. Both varieties have single and double petals. They can also be classified according to the size of flowers, as large, medium, and small. The best kind, however, is the fragrant, single.petaled variety with flowers of from medium to large size.

There is a variety, found both among

white and red Flowering Japanese Apricots, whose branches have a particular grace in that they droop down, for which reason they are called 'Shidare-Ume' (Drooping Japanese Apricot). This variety is highly prized by some lovers of *bonsai*.

Material tree Formerly, an old tree uprooted from the mountains was used as the material tree. However, in Japan at present, such a tree is no longer available. So, either grafting is made on two-year old seedlings, or cuttings are used. In either case, the branches and roots are trimmed close and the tree is planted in the garden, to be given plentiful fertilizer in order to develop fine roots and branches. The tree is then dug up in autumn after it has shed its leaves, its branches and roots are trimmed close again, and then replanted to be given more fertilizer. By repeating this process over a period of two to three years, the trunk can be expected to grow quite thick and the general framework of the tree's shape is completed. It is then planted in the container, and by that time the tree is ready to put on several flower-buds.

Fertilizer application The best type of soil to be used in the container is a mixture of black loam, Kanuma soil, and coarse sand in the proportion of 6–2–2. The container should be an azalea-pot or shallow unglazed pottery. The best time for planting in the container is just after the flowering-season. At the time of planting, examine the shape of the tree carefully, cut off all unnecessary branches, and prune the tree while leaving two or three one-year old branches. Next, trim the fine roots short and then plant in a container with good water drainage.

The container must be placed in a place where there is both plenty of sunlight and air.

Water the plant as often as the surface of the soil in the container becomes dry. Water should be given plentifully, especially during budding-time and in summer. Start applying fertilizer only when approximately three weeks have passed after planting in the container. In case of liquid fertilizer, apply it two or three times a month. In case of solid fertilizer to be deposited on the surface of the soil, apply it once a month or so.

Fertilizer should be applied until about the end of the hot season.

The fertilizer to be applied until early summer should be only rapeseed cake. Liquid fertilizer should be weak and applied several times. Later, fertilizer of an animal nature should be applied mixed with a small amount of superphosphate. This fertilizer should be somewhat stronger, for it will make the plant put on many flowers.

Pinching buds New densely grown buds or unnecessary shoots which tend to grow weak and long should be pinched from the base as soon as they appear. As for the shoots which have been left, only the tips of those should be pinched that tend to grow too long. This pinching should be done about the time when the leaves have more or less hardened. If new buds are pinched indiscriminately, the result will be that the branches do not grow thick. Moreover, the branches tend to wither in winter, and there will be only a few flowers. Hence the great care needed in pinching buds.

Arranging by wiring At about the time of pinching the buds, the branches should be arranged by wiring with paper-wrapped wires. However, this is not always necessary. In fact, in the case of old branches or trunks, this branch-arranging should be done rather by suspending the branches.

Control of injurious insects Common insects are stem borers, caterpillars that infest 'Ume' (Flowering Japanese Apricot), aphids, scales, etc. These can best be eradicated by spraying suitable insecticides at the time of their outbreak.

Pruning branches The best time for pruning the branches is in spring when the new buds have appeared. After studying the overall appearance of the tree, cut off all unnecessary branches. Then prune to a proper length the branches which have developed in the previous year by looking at the condition of the flower-buds.

How to treat parts which have been cut All decayed parts should be carved off during winter from trunks and thick branches with cuts. These places should be carved thoroughly smooth, then covered by either adhesive plaster or wax-cloth.

Cold protection in winter 'Ume' (Flowering Japanese Apricot) is a tree that withstands cold well. However, in winter, the branches sometimes wither and the leaves are often injured. So, in winter, after the plant has been exposed to two or three light frosts, it should be taken inside where there is plenty of light, or put in a frost-proof shelter. If the plant is watered during this period and the temperature is maintained at 60–70 degrees Farenheit, the early blossoming varieties will begin to put on flowers in about a month's time.

Points to bear in mind during blossom time The tree should be given plenty of sunlight, water and air. Before the flowers open, the tree should be sprinkled as often as possible. If there are too many flower-buds, they should be thinned out. Those flowers which have faded should be nipped off so that they will not develop into fruits.

Transplanting 'Ume' (Flowering Japanese Apricot) should be transplanted once a year, after the blossom season is over. At this time, all the branches should be pruned except those one-year old branches which are to be grown so that new branches can put on flower-buds.

Plants that may be treated in the same manner as 'Ume' (Flowering Japanese Apricot) 'Sanzashi' (Nippon Hawthorn), 'Kaidō' (Showy Crab Apple), etc., are typical ones.

Boke (Flowering Quince)

Characteristics Unlike large trees, such as the pines and 'Ume' (Flowering Japanese Apricot), 'Boke' (Flowering Quince) is a bush that develops branches and leaves close to the ground. So it is suited for growing in a cluster, representing its appearance in nature, than for growing as a *bonsai* representing a huge old tree. 'Boke' (Flowering Quince) is a hardy tree and has a life span over a hundred years. Buds appear very vigorously, so that they can be pinched without fear of overdoing. It puts forth numerous branches with a primitive elegance. And the flowers which begin to bloom in winter and continue into spring are varicolored. There are some varieties that put on large fruits whose appearance on the branches enhances the beauty of the tree considerably. It is suitable for growing as a *bonsai*. Moreover, it is an easy tree to grow, too, so that all *bonsai*-growers should try to have at least one 'Boke' (Flowering Quince).

Varieties There are various varieties of 'Boke' (Flowering Quince), but the kinds most commonly used for purposes of growing as *bonsai* are the following:

(1) 'Kusa-Boke'. Less than 1 meter in height, with thin branches and thorns. The flowers are single-petaled, ranging from crimson to white in color. It bears a lot of fruits.

(2) 'Chōjubai'. This is a 'Boke' (Flowering Quince) of a dwarfed nature. There are two kinds, those that bear red flowers and those that bear white. The tree has flowers almost all the year round.

(3) 'Kan-boke'. This is a variety that blooms very early in the year. The commonest kind are single-petaled with red flowers, but there are also those with white flowers, red with white stripes, and those with light brown stripes.

(4) 'Boke' (Flowering Quince) that blooms in spring. There are numerous kinds. They all have thick branches which are not too dense, and the flowers are brilliantly-colored, single-petaled, and large. The blossom-time is spring.

Material tree In the case of 'Kusa-Boke', the material tree may be uprooted from the mountains or fields, while in the case of 'Chōjubai', grafted trees are used. As for 'Kan-Boke' and 'Boke' that blooms in spring, plants propagated by division or cuttings may be used. In both cases, it must be remembered that 'Boke' (Flowering Quince) are susceptible to nematoda or parasites that cause warts to develop near the roots, and therefore in selecting the material tree, care should be used to choose a disease-free tree.

Soil and fertilizer The soil in the container should be either black loam and red clay, mixed with approximately 30% of coarse sand. The best time for planting the tree

Kan-Boke (Japanese Quince)

Kan-Boke (Japanese Quince)
Miniature *Bonsai*

in the container is in autumn after the leaves have fallen. However, so long as the planting is done while the buds are still hard, it may be done in early spring just as well. As for the place where 'Boke' (Flowering Quince) should be put, the same rules apply as in the case of 'Ume' (Flowering Japanese Apricot). However, in mid-summer, the direct sunlight in the afternoon should be avoided. Watering should be the same as in the case of any other plant. Water the leaves as well only immediately after transplanting, during budding-time and when the buds begin to open. Fertilizer application is the same as for 'Ume' (Japanese Flowering Apricot).

Summer Pruning During the growing stage new buds sprout all the time, which should be pruned as soon as they appear. Those that have been left are allowed to grow thick and long. When the new twigs have become more or less hard, all leaves with the exception of a few should be closely trimmed. This causes the secondary buds to sprout vigorously. These secondary shoots should be allowed to grow long and thick.

Trimming the Branches The secondary branches, that is, those which have developed from secondary buds, are allowed to grow thick, and in autumn, after the leaves have fallen, they should be trimmed to suitable lengths observing the condition of the flowerbuds. At the same time, all branches that have lost their vitality or are too dense grown or withered branches should be trimmed, to ensure the general shape of the tree. So wiring should be done only when unavoidable. Usually, it should be enough to arrange the branches by mere trimming.

Transplanting Transplanting should be done once a year in autumn after the leaves have fallen.

Fuji (Japanese Wisteria)

Characteristics As 'Fuji' (Japanese Wisteria) is a climbing plant, it may seem unfit for growing as *bonsai*. However, it can be used for *bonsai* by cutting the tendrils short. It has salient features of its own—a thick and graceful trunk with numerous bends, thick, short branches that grow sparsely from the trunk, and long tufts of flowers that show themselves from underneath the verdure of its young leaves. The flowering-season is late spring. The plant is comparatively easy to grow and it enjoys an extremely long life.

Varieties There are more than twenty varieties of 'Fuji' (Japanese Wisteria), and the flowers range in color from purple to white. The flowers may be single- or double-petaled. The length of the tufts is usually about 30 cm., but there are some with tufts as long as 1 meter. Of these numerous varieties, that which is most commonly used for *bonsai* is *Yama-Fuji* which has a thick coarse bark. Its flowers are white or purple, single-petaled, and large. The tufts are not so long, ranging from 15 to 20 cm. in length.

Material Tree If a mother tree is obtained from the mountains or fields, its roots will not develop so easily. On the other hand, seedlings from seeds take about twenty years before they bear any blosoms. Accordingly, the usual method is to use a grafted tree, which bears flowers in a short time. However, even in the case of grafted trees, if these are transplanted into a container, the flowers will be very long in coming. The best way, therefore, is to use young trees from four to five years of age with flower-buds.

In purchasing a grafted tree, give attention to the following points:

(1) The grafting should be done on the stock as close to the roots as possible. The joint should be thoroughly healed so that it is inconspicuous;

(2) The tree must be healthy, free of nematodes at the root and disease-free.

(3) The tree should not be too tall, and it should have numerous branches in its lower parts.

(4) It should be a well-known variety and should have many flower-buds.

The best time to purchase a plant is in autumn after the leaves have fallen.

Method of planting In the case of a grafted

tree, prune its tendrils and roots short enough so that it can be planted in the container. Plant it temporarily in a ground to develop its root system. After about a month, the tree will have numerous white roots. At a suitable time, dig up the plant, being careful not to hurt the roots, then plant it in a container filled with an mixture of equal parts of black loam and red clay. Water drainage must be satisfactory.

Upon completing the planting, give plenty of water and then put it in a cold-proof shelter. Water the tree and roots once every day to ensure better root growth. With the coming of the warm spring in the following year, put the plant outdoors.

Fertilizer application Apply weak liquid fertilizer of rapeseed cake at the end of the flowering-season, alternating it with solid fertilizer deposited on the soil surface. When the new vines have developed and the leaves have hardened, apply fertilizer two or three times. This fertilizer should be deposited on the soil surface and should consist of rapeseed cake, mixed with bone meal and a small amount of superphosphate. In autumn, give the plant rather strong liquid fertilizer consisting of rapeseed cake, then deposit some fertilizer on the soil surface. Both types of fertilizer should be given at least once, and after that, no more fertilizer. It is said that 'Fuji' (Japanese Wisteria) requires from three to four times as much fertilizer as most *bonsai*.

Watering should be just enough to moisten the soil surface thoroughly. In mid-summer, a plant which so far has been watered two to three times a day should be watered only once in two days. This causes the tips of the vines and leaves to look withered during the daytime. When this happens, place the container in water and let it absorb all the water it needs. This process should be repeated two or three times at intervals of five to six days. The result will be that the vines will stop growing and the buds will become flower-buds. This is how grafted wisteria trees can be made to bear flowers.

The tree shape and branch-arranging By nature, 'Fuji' (Japanese Wisteria) is a plant that grows by clinging to other objects. Its branches are sparse, its leaves large, and its flowers hang down in tufts. Because of the peculiar nature of the plant, it is best suited to grow in the form of a cascade or semi-cascade *bonsai*.

The trunk grows obliquely or bends to one side. The branches must be distributed evenly on both the left and right sides, so that the appearance of the plant may be properly arranged. For such arrangement, the resilient branches of 'Fuji' (Japanese Wisteria) are particularly suited. The trunk and branches should be arranged by wiring or suspended in spring when the new buds begin to appear. In the case of new vines, use paper-wrapped wires for wiring after the leaves have more or less hardened. As the vines of 'Fuji' (Japanese Wisteria) have a tendency to entwine themselves clockwise, any wires that are applied should be wound in the same direction, and the branches must be bent while twisting them in the same direction.

Trimming the new vines When 'Fuji' (Japanese wisteria) is grown in a container, the vines naturally tend to become shorter. However, if the plant is young, the vines will show great vitality even when the plant is in a container. Trimming the vines indiscriminately jeopardizes its growth and prevents the bearing of flower-buds. To prevent this, allow the vines to grow until about the time the leaves are more or less hardened, then pinch the tips of the vines or bend them. In autumn, after the leaves have fallen, leave one to three vines, and trim the rest.

All unnecessary branches should be cut off immediately after the flowering-season.

Clipping the beans When the flowering-season is over, 'Fuji (Japanese Wisteria) bears legume-like fruits. The sight of these legumes hanging from the tree has a peculiar beauty of its own, but if too many of them are allowed to grow, they weaken the plant. So just leave a few and cut off the rest as soon as possible.

Transplanting Transplanting should be done every year immediately after the flowering-season. At this time, withered or aged roots should be cut off, leaving only the vigorous roots. These roots should be bundled up and the tree planted in the container again.

Momiji (Japanese Maple)

Characteristics This is a hardy tree able to withstand extremes of heat and cold. It can endure trimming quite well and has a long life span in a container. The trunk develops firm roots and rises gracefully from the ground. The appearance of the trunk as well as the bark has an elegance all its own. Branches grow densely with delicate tips, giving the tree a soft and graceful appearance. The shape of the leaves resembles the palm of the hand with points like the teeth of a saw. The tree is beautiful to look at in spring when the buds come out, in summer when the leaves are green, but most of all the tree is an object of surpassing beauty when the leaves have turned scarlet. The tree is also extremely beautiful to look at after the leaves have fallen, for it reminds one of a winter landscape in nature.

The tree is particularly suitable for growing as *bonsai* as it can be made to take almost any desired shape. The process of growing, too, is very simple, and long care bestowed on the plant will be richly repaid by increasing its value as *bonsai*. Ranking only next to the pine-tree and 'Ume' (Flowering Japanese Apricot), 'Momiji' (Japanese Maple) is one of the most important of *bonsai* plants.

Varieties There are many varieties, but for *bonsai*, varieties with small, dense leaves are preferred. Such varieties are the 'Yama-Momiji', 'Seigen', etc.

Points to bear in mind in growing bonsai The material tree of 'Momiji' (Japanese Maple) may be uprooted in the mountains, but seedlings, grafted trees, trees obtained by layering, etc., may also be used. There are various ways of growing these as *bonsai* and of arranging their shape.

However, the most important thing to remember in growing 'Momiji' (Japanese Maple) as *bonsai* is to build up a shape that is both graceful and delicate. The trunk must be round, without scars, and straight. The branches must be arranged gracefully and delicately, with almost a feminine beauty.

In order to grow such *bonsai*, the best thing to do is to start with a seedling. In the following pages the technique of growing *bonsai* from a seedling best suited for beginners will be explained. The technique is also the most up-to-date.

How to plant the seeds The seeds should be fully ripened ones from 'Yama-Momiji', which should have small, dense leaves and is beautiful in autumn when the leaves change color. The seeds should be dried in the shade and then immersed in water. Selecting those which have sunk to the bottom, and plant them immediately.

The best place to plant the seeds is in a flat or shallow container. At the bottom of the container, there should be a layer of coarse sand. Then put in lumps of red clay about the size of millet grains. After this, fill about one-third of the container with small pebbles that have dents in them so that they will be stable. Instead of pebbles, one may also use earth obtained from a swamp, kneaded into lumps the shape of cones.

Scatter the seeds in a thin layer on top of the pebbles or lumps of swamp soil. Then put in enough earth so that the seeds will be concealed. Water gently with a sprinkler. Place the container in the shade.

Growing a young tree Watering is necessary only when there is danger of drying. Dew and rain are sufficient. The seeds will sprout the next spring. The young plants should be put outdoors when two or three leaves have opened, in a place where the sun shines on the plants in the morning but not in the afternoon. Water should be applied as often as the soil gets dry.

Weak liquid fertilizer should be applied from time to time. Closely grown plants should be thinned out so that the leaves do not overlap. During the summer, on hot days, the container should be placed in semi-

Illustration Showing How 'Momiji' (Japanese Maple) and 'To-Kaede' (Trident Maple) are Planted on Rocks.

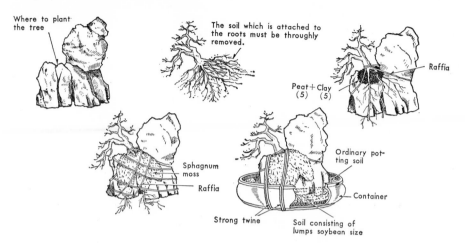

The purpose of a *bonsai* on a rock is to reproduce the natural appearance of a tree on a rock. The best time for planting this type of *bonsai* is in spring just before the buds sprout. 'Momiji' (Japanese Maple) and 'Tō-Kaede' (Trident Maple) are both suited for this type of *bonsai*. The same method may be used for either tree. Beginners are urged to try with either plant.

Explanation of the Illustration.

(a) *Rock for use in planting a bonsai on a rock.* The rock must be one that has an attractive shape, neither too large nor too small, and one that is stable. It must have a dent, a groove or a crack in which the tree may be planted easily. As for the color of the rock, one of a dark and subdued color should be chosen.

(b) *Tree for use in planting a bonsai on a rock.* Whether the tree chosen is 'Momiji' (Japanese Maple) or 'Tō-Kaede' (Trident Maple), be sure that it is a young tree with more or less a definite shape. Its lower branches must be thick and hanging down, and its fine roots must be numerous and long. All the soil adhering to the roots should be removed.

(c) *How to plant the tree.* Apply a thick coating of a mixture of equal parts of peat and clay kneaded with water on the dent in the rock. Place the tree on this mixture, then divide the roots into three or four bunches, and let the tree stand on the rock in as graceful a position as possible. Use raffia and other material to tie the base of the trunk firmly to the rock.

(d) *Distribution of the roots.* Distribute the main roots, one by one, down the cracks or grooves in the rock, toward its base. Smear the mixture of peat and clay on the rock so as to make the root cling firmly. After all the main roots have been attached to the rock, follow the same procedure to secure the smaller roots to the rock. Lastly cover the roots with a thin coating of sphagnum moss. Tie everything down with raffia.

(e) After the tree has been planted on the rock, choose a shallow container that is somewhat larger than the rock, and plant the tree in the container, rock and all. Plant the tree as shown in the illustration. Any roots whose tips have been left unfastened to the rock should be buried in the container, taking care not to hurt them and at the same time, seeing to it that the root ends are planted in a graceful manner.

After the tree and rock have been placed in the container, tie the rock to the container by means of twine so that the rock will not move. Pour water on the plant in sufficient quantities. After this, treat the plant as you would any other tree that has been recently transplanted.

shade where there is a good breeze. When the time comes for the leaves to fall, the plants will be from 10 to 20 cm. tall.

In winter, either place the container indoors or bury the container in the ground to give protection against frost and cold. Watering should not be neglected during this period so that the soil in the container does not become dry. When the weather becomes warm again in spring, the container should be placed on a shelf, so that the plants will be exposed to sunshine all day. Fertilizer should be applied the same as in the preceding year.

How to arrange the leaves In the second year, the terminal bud will first appear, followed by the appearance of lateral buds in the nodes in the upper part. The leaves on 'Momiji' (Japanese Maple) grow in pairs, one on the left side and one on the right. So, the lateral-buds, like the leaves, also grow in pairs.

When the young shoots become about 20 cm. long, the top of the terminal-bud should be pinched in order to prevent the tree from further growth, and at the same time, to stimulate the development of the lateral-buds. The lateral-buds, if allowed to grow in pairs, will make the tree unsightly. Hence, they should be pinched so that they will grow alternately, one on the left side, then the next one on the right, etc. All unnecessary lateral-buds should be nipped as soon as possible, so that the basic form of the tree might be gradually formed.

This is the method of growing not for a single plant, but for a group of plants in the container in a cluster on a rock or hill.

Hence, if the branches of the young trees are uniformly arranged, the result will be monotonous. The trees then have to be arranged according as they are long or short, thick or thin, bent or straight, so that the whole creates an illusion of a cluster of 'Momiji' (Japanese Maple) growing in perspective on a rock or hill. Of course, all unnecessary seedlings must be cut off, while those that have an unpleasant appearance should be corrected by wiring.

Those saplings which have grown on the outside of the cluster should have their inside branches pruned and their outside

branches left. Those seedlings in the middle should have their lower branches thinned, and their thick branches made to grow alternately to the left and to the right, while their small branches should be made to grow forward and backward.

Principles of fertilizer application The young trees should be placed in a place where there is plenty of sunlight, fresh air, and breeze. In summer, they should be placed where the sun shines for three or four hours in the morning, after which they should be placed where it is shady and cool. In winter, they should be placed in an cold-proof shelter or in a room to protect them against the cold. It should be watered as in the case of all other plants. Beside normal watering in spring when the buds appear, syringing should be done once a day, and in summer, once in the morning and once in the evening.

During the growing period of the seedlings, liquid fertilizer and composite fertilizer should be used, always taking into consideration the color of the leaves and the general condition of the plants. Any insects infesting the leaves or branches should be eradicated.

Bud-Pinching The terminal-bud should be cut off when it has attained a height of about 10 cm., leaving about two nodes. The lateral-buds, with the exception of those that are to be left for thickening should be pruned when they have grown about three nodes, leaving just one. Before long, the secondary buds will appear, at which time, leave one that is in good condition. Let this shoot grow till it is about two nodes long. Leave one node and nip it off. Pinching the new buds in this manner before they become too thick is the secret of making a delicately shaped tree that has no scars.

Wiring When the leaves have more or less hardened, the branches should be wired with paper-wrapped wires. It is possible to arrange even four to five-year old trunks and branches, but care must be used because 'Momiji' (Japanese Maple) is a tree with a soft bark into which wire can easily cut in.

Leaf-Cutting The purpose of leaf-cutting is to make the leaves of 'Yama-Momiji' even smaller and denser, and to make their tips more delicate, softer and closer. The technique of leaf-cutting has been explained above.

Transplanting If 'Momiji' (Japanese Maple) is transplanted once every year, it stimulates the plant's growth to excess, causing the tree shape to get out of control. The branches will become rough, and the leaves large and sparse. Therefore, transplanting should be done only once in three or four years. When transplanting 'Momiji' (Japanese Maple), make sure that it is removed from the container without taking it apart from the rock or the block of peat. Next, remove some of the soil from the roots, prune the tips of the roots and all unnecessary branches, and then plant it again in a flat container. The soil in the container should consist of five parts of black loam, three of red clay, and two of coarse sand. It is important to have a layer of coarse sand at the bottom of the pot to ensure good water-drainage.

If the method here described is followed, the tree will become a fairly presentable *bonsai* in about three years. After about ten years, the thick roots will twine together, the trunks and branches will put on an appearance of age, and the *bonsai* will give the viewer such joy as no single tree can give. Other trees that may be treated in the same manner as 'Momiji' (Japanese Maple) are 'To-Kaede' (Trident Maple), 'Soro', (Loose-Flower Hornbeam), etc.

To-Kaede (Trident Maple) planted on the rock.

Umemodoki (Ilex serrata var. Sieboldii)

Characteristics This plant puts on countless berries about the size of soya beans of coral red all over its twigs starting in late autumn and continuing well on into the winter. Of the many types of fruit-bearing plants used as *bonsai*, this is an outstanding plant that has always enjoyed unsurpassed popularity.

Varieties Besides the one variety stated above, there are others, such as those that bear white berries, and also a third kind that bears berries of both pink and white. Both of these varieties are used as *bonsai*, but the ordinary kind bearing red berries easily surpasses all other varieties in popularity.

Mother Tree As the material tree, either a wild tree in the mountains or one that grows

Umemodoki (Ilex serrata, var. Sieboldii)

Umemodoki (Deciduous Holly; Ilex serrata var. Sieboldii)

in the garden may be used provided it has the makings of *bonsai* and shapely branches. One may dig up such a tree, but in most cases, one starts with a seedling. The former often happens to have wart-like swellings at the places where the trunk or branches have been cut, while the latter has the disadvantage that the grower has to wait ten years or more before the plant bears berries.

For beginners, it is better not to go to a great deal of trouble looking for and growing material tree, but to buy a *bonsai* which has a definite shape and which already bears berries. It involves less expense, and one can start enjoying the tree from the very next day.

In the following paragraphs, the technique of growing 'Umemodoki' (Ilex Serrata, var. Seiboldii) and other measures to be observed in taking care of the plant will be explained.

Fertilizer application, etc. The plant should be placed on an outdoor shelf. In winter only, it should be placed in a place where the cold wind does not blow and where it is free from frost or snow. Watering should be the same as in the case of any ordinary plant, but it needs more water from the time its flowers begin to open until the time the plant puts on berries. Lack of water during this time causes the plant not to bear berries.

During the growing season, it should be given weak liquid fertilizer once or twice a month. After the summer, the plant does not require so much fertilizer as do other plants that bear large fruits.

Pinching New buds which have begun to develop, and unnecessary buds should be pinched off as soon as possible, but those which have been left should be allowed to grow until about the time the leaves harden. Then, taking the arrangement of the branches into consideration, the shoots should be pinched to about 3 to 6 cm. in length.

Presently, the secondary buds will appear. Of these secondary buds, pinch off those that are unnecessary, and let the rest grow.

Arranging the shape of the tree by wiring The new buds left in order to grow into branches should be arranged by wiring with paper-wrapped wires about the time the leaves have hardened, cutting off only their tips. It should be borne in mind when doing this that 'Umemodoki' (Ilex serrata var. Seiboldii) is a plant which snaps easily. So it is safer not to give it water for a day or two prior to the wiring. Again, the branches should not be bent at an acute angle. When the wiring is over, give plenty of water so that it can regain its vitality.

Transplanting Transplanting should be done once a year in spring just before the buds come out. At the same time, the branches which grew the year before should be pruned in order to arrange the tree's shape. When an old branch has been cut off, be sure that the place where the cut has been made is carved smooth and wax cloth applied in the form of a cross. As for the soil for transplanting, the best kind is a mixture of 7 parts of black loam with 3 of red clay or 'Kanuma' soil.

Picking the Berries The red berries of 'Umemodoki' (Ilex serrata, var. Seiboldii) become even redder if they are exposed once or twice to light frost. It is better to bring the plant indoors only after that to enjoy viewing the red berries. However, if the berries are allowed to stay too long on the tree, they exhaust the plant, with the result that there will be fewer berries the next year. Therefore, all berries should be picked after about a month.

Shimpaku (Chinese Juniper)

Characteristics This is a very hardy tree that survives for hundreds of years in a container. When the trunk becomes very old, the bark falls off almost completely and the wood part decays, leaving only the core of the tree. Even under such adverse conditions, the tree manages to survive on the little remaining bark, giving its viewers an impression of venerable grandeur. The branches are fine and dense, and its leaves

Shimpaku (Chinese Juniper) " Moyō-Ki " Bonsai which has crooked trunks. This tree was found cn a cliff and treated just a little.

Shimpaku (Chinese Juniper) with beautiful *Sharimiki* (trunks which lost most bark and weathered). This was found in nature and is 250 years old.

are green, short and rope-shaped. The foliage which covers the tree is a source of enjoyment to the viewer, no less than the shapely trunk. The reason why 'Shimpaku' is so highly prized as *bonsai* is that it always shows great vigor in spite of its age, and the tenacity with which it survives gives the tree a venerable appearance.

Varieties There are many varieties related to 'Shimpaku'. There is a variety with leaves like those of 'Sugi' (Japanese Cedar), and branches that crawl on the ground, called 'Haibyaku-Shin' (Creeping Japanese Juniper). There is another variety which is planted in gardens, called 'Kaizuka-Ibuki,' a third variety with yellow variegated leaves called 'Ōgon Ibuki' (Juniperus Chineusis, var. aureoglobosa), and a fourth variety of an extreme dwarfed nature, used as a border for flower-beds, called 'Tama-Ibuki' (J. Chineusis, var. globosa). However, none of these varieties are suitable for growing as *bonsai,* except 'Shimpaku'.

Mother tree The best kind of material tree would be a plant two or three hundred years old, found on some precipice in the deep mountains or an unexplored valley—a tree that has withstood the austerities of all weathers, and whose branches and trunk are bent or partially bleached.

However, such old trees are so hard to obtain. Hence, the usual custom is to raise a material tree by cutting in summer.

Of course, a tree like this cannot be compared with an old tree that has been uprooted from the mountains, but it can be made to take almost any shape. If it is planted with a rock and grown as a cascade style of *bonsai,* it will develop into a beautiful *bonsai* in a few years.

Growing The plant should be placed where there is plenty of sunlight and breeze. The air must be fresh, and at night, the plant must be exposed to the night dew. Watering should be the same as in the case of any other plant. Besides, the leaves should be syringed twice a day till summer, once in the morning and once in the evning. In winter once a day is quite enough. In doing this, it is important that the water reaches not only both sides of the leaves, but also all the branches and the trunk.

Weak liquid fertilizer of rapeseed cake is applied during the budding season in spring and during the growing season once a week. No strong fertilizer should be given under any circumstances. With excessive fertilizer, the branches grow too long and the tree becomes unshapely.

Pinching The new buds of 'Shimpaku' are three-pronged and they appear in spring and in autumn. The central bud should be pinched before it becomes hard. A day or two later, the two buds remaining on either side should be pinched in the same way.

If the buds are pinched in such a way immediately after their appearance, the secondary buds will appear in four or five days from the base of the places where the buds have been pinched. These secondary buds, too, should be pinched in the same way. The secondary buds, then, are followed by the third buds. Hence, in the case of 'Shimpaku', it is necessary to repeat the process of pinching all through the budding-season. This is the secret of increasing the branches and of making the bud-tips fine and dense and beautiful.

Trimming the branches When the bud-tips of 'Shimpaku' become too dense, the lower branches and also those in the middle become impeded in their development. The result is a top-heavy appearance. An overgrown tree is a very unsightly thing. So the branches should be pinched at least once a year.

The best time for trimming is in spring before the buds come out. Branches which point upward, those which are growing vigorously and those which have grown too long should be pruned. Other branches that should be cut are withered and dense branches. Whenever branches are pruned, make sure that there is a small branch or a young branch under the branch that is cut off.

How to dispose of cedar-like leaves It sometimes happens that 'Shimpaku' develops cedar-like leaves. This is a very common phenomenon seen in trees which have lost their vitality, but which, upon applying fertilizer, regain their strength. These cedar-like leaves greatly reduce the value of 'Shimpaku' as *bonsai,* so that the tree must be transplanted at a suitable time and given proper fertilizer. Merely cutting off the cedar leaves does not do any good. If the cedar leaves are to be cut off, it is better to do so after the tree has sufficiently recovered its vitality.

How to prevent leaf-burn In mid-summer, if the tree is exposed to a very strong sun, and water is short, leaf-burn takes place. In order to prevent this, the plant should not be exposed to the direct sun in the afternoon in mid-summer, and it should be given plentiful water.

Transplanting 'Shimpaku' should be transplanted once every three years in spring when the buds have begun to appear. The soil for transplanting should be a mixture of 7 parts of red clay and 3 of coarse sand. There should be a thin layer of crushed lime stone at the bottom of the container.

Toshō (Needle Juniper)

Characteristics This is a hardy tree that survives a long time. The trunk is hard and straight, and is suitable for growing as *bonsai* of "Chokkan" style with a single straight trunk. Especially an old tree having dense needle leaves of dark green with short white lines has an aspect of grandeur that few other *bonsai* can boast of. It can also be grown as a miniature *bonsai*. Growing is simple.

Varieties There are many varieties related to 'Toshō' (Needle Juniper), such as 'Yore-Nezu' (Juniperus rigida, var. filiformis) whose leaves are twisted spirally, 'Hai-Nezu' (Shore Juniper) whose branches and trunk crawl on the ground, 'Shidare-Nezu' the tips of whose branches droop down, etc. But none of these varieties can compare with 'Toshō' (Needle Juniper) as a tree for growing as *bonsai*.

Material Tree Usually, an old tree is uprooted from a crack in a rock in the mountains, or a young tree is uprooted in spring around budding time, and then grown in the garden for a year or two. Of course, if one does not mind that the plant is slow in putting out roots, cuttings or trees obtained by layering may be used.

Planting The best soil for planting is a mixture of coarse sand with 30 to 40% red clay. The container should be one of unglazed pottery of medium depth. Have a layer of gravel or lumpy earth at the bottom to ensure good water drainage. In the case of an old tree, the trunk should be cut off at a suitable height before the tree is planted. The tip should be made into '*jin*'—a top which is dead and weathered—thereby adding to the elegance of the *bonsai*.

Growing Syringe the leaves with water frequently until the roots have developed. Start giving fertilizer only after the roots are developed. The place for putting the plant is the same as for 'Shimpaku'. For watering the plant, syringing of the leaves with water is considered the best method. The fertilizer is the same as for 'Kuro-Matsu' (Japanese Black Pine). Too much fertilizer causes excessive growth of the branches and leaves.

Toshō (Needle Juniper) " Netsunagari " (Root-Connected Style)

Pinching The technique of pinching is the same as for 'Sugi' (Japanese Cedar). While the new buds continue to appear, pinching with the fingers should be repeated as often as necessary. The use of shears for pinching is harmful.

Arranging by wiring Arranging by wiring should be carried out on new twigs when the leaves have more or less hardened, and on young trunks and branches, in spring before the buds appear. Use paper-wrapped wires for the new twigs. As for the others, wrap raffia around those parts to be bent, and then apply bare wire. At the same time, cut off all unnecessary branches and arrange the tree's shape.

Carving Carving is done on the decayed parts of a trunk, or when it is desired that the top part of the trunk should be made into 'jin', or again, when the tip of a branch is to be made into 'jin' by removing the bark. All carving is done in winter.

Transplanting Transplanting is done once every three or four years when the new buds begin to appear. The soil for planting is as explained above. Change the container for a permanent one when the tree has taken a more or less definite shape.

Keyaki (Zelkova)

Characteristics Of the numerous types of deciduous trees, this is one which is prized for the grandeur and delicate beauty of its appearance in winter. It is suitable for growing as *bonsai,* as it can be made to take almost any desired shape. However, it is most suited for growing as a single straight-trunk *bonsai,* the technique of which is not difficult. It is a hardy tree that survives a long time in a container, and is beautiful to look at in spring when the buds come out, but even more so in autumn when the leaves put on their autumnal tints. Among the various kinds of deciduous trees used for *bonsai,* this tree ranks with 'Momiji' (Japanese Maple), 'To-Kaede' (Trident Maple), etc., and is surpassed only by 'Ume' (Flowering Japanese Apricot).

Varieties There are two varieties of 'Keyaki' —those that have a reddish tint when the new buds come out, and those that have a greenish tint. The former have smaller and denser leaves than the latter, and the autumnal tints, too, are more beautiful. Both varieties show great variation, depending on individual trees, in the size of the leaves and coarseness of the bark. For a choice *bonsai,* select a tree with reddish buds, small leaves, and bark that is thick, rugged and strong.

Material Tree For the material tree, one may use a cutting or a tree obtained by layering. Or again, one may uproot a tree from the mountains and fields. However, as 'Keyaki', like 'Momiji' (Japanese Maple), is a tree prized for its round, smooth trunk, rising vigorously from firm roots, it is best to start with a seedling that is a year old, especially because of its rapid growth. And in this way there is a better chance of growing a good *bonsai* which can be enjoyed in about 3 or 4 years.

Planting of a seedling Choose a healthy plant with reddish leaves. Dig it up when the leaves have barely begun to appear, prune the straight root short, and plant it in a small container. The soil for planting should be a mixture of red clay with 10 to 20% leaf mold and some river sand.

Growing When the plant has put out roots, place the container on a shelf and give water as in the case of any other plant. Use very weak liquid fertilizer once a week until autumn. Do not apply too much fertilizer. Do not allow the plant to grow too large, but rather let it grow into a compact shape. In mid-summer, avoid the direct afternoon sun.

Pinching The way of pinching differs even in the case of growing trees with straight trunks, depending on whether the branches are to grow in the form of tiers or in the shape of a broom. In the following paragraphs, the method of growing the branches into a broom-like shape will be explained, for this is the shape which is best suited for 'Keyaki'.

Let the terminal bud grow to about 15 to 21 cm. in length. The leaves become larger as they approach the tip. As there will always be a vigorous bud right next to a large leaf, one or two large leaves should be left at one-third or one-fourth of the desired height, and the part above should be cut off.

If the terminal bud is trimmed in this way, three to four lateral-buds will appear the following spring around the place where the cut was made. Select from among these buds the first branch, the second branch, and the third branch, which will form the basis of the tree shape. Then arrange the branches accordingly.

Cold-proof Shelter If 'Keyaki' planted in a small container is left outdoors in winter, the danger of withering at the tips of the buds will be invited. Therefore, the plant should be put into a shelter early. The inside of the shelter should not be sultry, and care must also be taken that the soil in the container never becomes dry.

Transplanting The following year, the plant should be transplanted into a container of a larger size, in spring before the buds come out. The soil for planting should be a mixture of 7 parts of red clay, 2 of leaf mold, and 1 of coarse sand. When transplanting, remove approximately half of the old soil, and replace it by new soil.

Care after transplanting Caring after trans-

Akashide (Loose-Flower Hornbeam)

planting is similar to that of the previous year. As for fertilizer, use a very weak liquid solution which should be used instead of water two or three times a week. Use a stronger solution once a week, starting in mid-summer and continuing until autumn.

Pinching Except for those new buds which are intended for growing into branches, leave 4 to 5 leaves out of the 6 or 7 leaves that have developed, and pinch their buds. Of the secondary buds, leave two to three leaves out of the four or five that have developed, and pinch the buds again. In the case of a tree with more or less a definite shape, leave two or three leaves and repeat the process of pinching two or three times rather early.

Arranging by wiring If the new twigs which are intended for growing into branches are left untended, the tips of the shoots hang down before the wood part of the twigs hardens, and the result is that growth is impeded. Therefore, the vitality of the tree should be maintained by pointing the new twigs upward by wiring with paper-wrapped wires as soon as possible before they start drooping.

Method of developing the roots The development of the roots is particularly important in growing 'Keyaki' with a single straight trunk. In order to improve the root development, the first step is to expose the plant to plenty of sunshine and to apply fertilizer. The second thing is to cover and protect the exposed roots with sphagnum moss.

Usually there is a thick branch on the side on which there is a thick root, so that a balance is maintained between the part above ground and that which is underground. So in order to expand the roots in all directions, branches should be so arranged as to spread in all directions, also.

Leaf-Cutting In the case of a tree with a completed shape, the leaves should be cut in order to increase the number of branches, and to ensure smaller and denser leaves. Leaf-cutting may be carried out three times a year on a very vigorous tree, but ordinarily, it is done only twice.

The first cutting should be done when the new twigs have reached a height of 12 to 15 cm. Two weeks before cutting the leaves, the tips of the new twigs should be pinched. This prevents the branches from growing longer, and fattens the leaves and stimulates the growth of the lateral-buds. Leave the stems of the leaves and cut off all the leaves.

The second cutting should be done about 6 weeks later. This time, begin the leaf-cutting immediately without pinching. Leaf-cutting is a drastic operation. So make sure that the tree is healthy before the operation. Care should be taken not to weaken the tree.

Other trees treated in the same manner as 'Keyaki' 'Akashide' (LooseFlower Hornbeam) 'Nire-Geyaki' (Chinese Elm), 'Enoki' (Japanese Hackberry), etc.

Kumashide (Carpinus carpinoides), Akashide (Loose-Flower Hornbeam)

Characteristics 'Kumashide' (Carpinus carpinoides) is related to 'Akashide' or 'Soro' (Loose-Flower Hornbeam). Their feature as *bonsai* is the enjoyment of the peculiar shape of the catkins. The bracts of flowers of 'Kumashide' (Carpinus carpinoides) are 4–5 cm. long and oval-shaped. 'Akashide' (Loose-Flower Hornbeam) bears bracts of flowers about 4 cm. in length, oblong in shape. The catkins of both 'Kumashide' and 'Akashide' are green, but the side exposed to the sun is faintly red. The way these catkins hang down from the branches is very elegant. The plants bear numerous catkins which last long. The leaves are large and coarse, and turn crimson in autumn in case of the former, while the leaves of the latter are dense and delicate and turn yellow in autumn.

Both are hardy plants, suitable for *bonsai*. Usually, these trees are grown into straight single trees, but they may also be used for combining with rocks. Growing is easy and the plant has a long life-span and is beautiful to look at in spring when the buds come out, in autumn when the leaves are either crimson or yellow and also in winter as winter-trees.

Material tree Young trees are uprooted from the mountains for material trees. The uprooting should be done in autumn after the leaves have fallen in warm districts, but in cold districts, it should be done in spring before the appearance of the buds.

Growing Cut short the straight root, trim the trunk and branches, then plant the tree in a small container with soil of red clay mixed with 20% of coarse sand. As for the place to put the container and the technique of watering, follow the same directions as for 'Keyaki'.

About three weeks after the plant has been transplanted into the container, apply very weak liquid fertilizer instead of water once every week. Continue this until autumn. Pinch the shoots that tend to grow too long after the leaves have more or less hardened. In the first year, however, let the shoots grow long so as to stimulate the development of the fine roots. Take cold-proof measures in winter.

Transplanting Transplanting should be done once every year, in spring before the buds come out. The soil for transplanting should be a mixture of 5 parts of black loam, 3 of red clay and 2 of coarse sand. Another possible mixture is 7 parts of red clay, 2 of leaf mold and 1 of coarse sand. Over-grown branches should be properly trimmed keeping balance with the total appearance of the tree.

Growing as a rule is the same as for the preceding year. However, the application of liquid fertilizer may be done with a stronger solution. From time to time, solid fertilizer might be deposited on the soil instead of liquid fertilizer. When the tree has more or less taken on a definite shape, apply an increased amount of phosphate and potash to stimulate flower-bearing.

Pinching Pinching should not be done on a weak tree, but on vigorous trees, it may be done two to three times in early spring and mid-summer.

Arranging the tree shape by wiring Although new twigs and young branches may be scarred by wiring, the scars can be healed by arrange the branches. However, remove them before they cut into the branches and trunk.

Leaf-Cutting Leaf-cutting should be avoided as much as possible because of its unfavorable effect on flower-bearing. However, it should be encouraged in the case of 'Akashide' (Loose-Flower Hornbeam) whose purpose is the enjoyment of the new buds in spring and the tints of autumn, provided the tree is one that has not yet bloomed and is in a vigorous state. With such trees, syringe the leaves not only after the leaf-cutting but during mid-summer to prevent leaf-burn as well as to wash and clean the leaves.

Trimming the branches The branches should be trimmed at the time of transplanting. However, as the flower catkins appear at the tips of the new twigs, the branches should be left rather long at first. Find out if there are any flowers or not, then cut to a suitable length.

Buna (Japanese Beech)

Characteristics Though this is a deciduous tree, it does not become completely bare in late autumn. Its brown withered leaves remain on the tree throughout the winter. The leaves fall only when the sharp-pointed new buds appear. This characteristic makes it a favorite with many *bonsai*-growers. It is hardy and survives a long time. Growing is easy, too.

Varieties Of the many varieties of 'Buna', the species best suited for growing as *bonsai* is that called 'Inu-Buna' (Faguls japonica). 'Inu-Buna' are further divided into two kinds, those with green buds and those with red. The leaves are of various kinds, round, small, large, spear-shaped and some shaped like those of bamboo grass. The best type is that with red buds and small round leaves.

Kumashide (Carpinus Carpinoides)

Buna (Japanese Beech) showing the fine bark of the trunk.

Material tree Seedlings and trees obtained by layering are used as material trees, but in general, a young tree or a sapling uprooted from the mountains is used. In the case of a young tree, its trunk is cut off at a height of about 30 cm, and its branches are trimmed before uprooting.

Transplanting The best soil for transplanting is an equal mixture of coarse sand with black loam. The container should be rather deep, with coarse soil at the bottom, less coarse soil in the middle, and finer soil at the top, to ensure good water-drainage.

Growing Place the container on an outdoor shelf in spring and autumn. In mid-summer, place the container in a cool place where the sun will shine for two or three hours in the morning, and transfer it to a shady place for the rest of the day. In winter, put the container in a shelter to protect it against the cold.

Give plenty of water all the time. Water should be sprinkled on the leaves from the time the leaves harden until the end of summer. Liquid fertilizer consisting of rapeseed cake is applied together with solid fertilizer deposited on the soil, from spring after the appearance of the buds until the middle of autumn. Watch the color of the leaves to avoid the application of excessive fertilizer. With lack of either fertilizer or water, the leaves will not last until winter.

Let the new shoots grow long the first year. Pinch the tip of over-growth shoots.

Tree shape The tree shape should be ordinarily straight. 'Buna' (Japanese Beech), by nature does not develop roots so well, so better results are obtained if the trees are planted with rocks or in groups. In any case, the transplanting time is in spring before the buds come out.

Planting with rocks Select a shapely and stable rock—one that has cracks, grooves, and dents. A medium-sized rock which is easy to handle is preferable. Select a material tree with long fine roots.

First prepare a mixture of clay and sphagnum moss. Then cover the dents in the rock where the tree is to be planted with the said soil mixture. Next, divide the roots into three parts and place the plant over the dent and tie the roots down firmly to the rock with

twine. Then insert each of the tripartite roots into the grooves in the rock, starting at the top and working downwards. When the roots are inserted in the grooves, cover the rock with the same soil mixture and tie with twine.

After the tree has been planted on the rock, it should be placed, rock and all, in a flat container in an artistic manner. There should be plenty of coarse sand at the bottom of the container, over which the soil described above should be applied. The lower ends of the roots should be buried in the soil and if the roots do not reach the soil, apply a thick coating of sphagnum moss over it them.

After the tree is planted, give plenty of water over the entire plant. Keep the container in semi-shade until the roots develop fully. In the meantime, frequently syringe the leaves with water.

Pinching The new buds of 'Buna' grow vigorously. So over-grown buds should be pinched. There will be no secondary buds. Not only that, but the internodes will become great, and warts tend to develop at places where cuts have been made. So the young shoots should be pinched only once while they are still soft, leaving just one or two leaves.

Leaf-Cutting It is safer not to cut the leaves during the growing stage of the tree. Even in the case of a tree with a permanent shape, it is dangerous to cut the leaves every year. Cutting the leaves once every other year or so is sufficient.

Arranging by wiring Use paper-wrapped wires, and remove all wires three months after the wiring at the latest. The reason is that the bark is soft and that the tree grows thick very quickly. A tree whose branches have been arranged by wiring will show a tendency of not sucking up water so well as before. So it should be placed in the shade, and the under sides of the leaves should be moistened with sprayed water.

Trimming the branches A tree that has been transplanted should have its branches trimmed, but the trimming of too many branches causes withering. So the buds should be pinched while they are still soft in order to prevent excessive·growth.

Buna (Japanese Beach),
Yose-ue (Cluster of trees)

Transplanting Transplanting is done once a year in spring. However, in the case of a rock-planted tree, transplanting is necessary only once in two or three years.

Other trees that may be treated in the same manner as 'Buna' 'Nara' (Small-Leafed Oak), 'Kunugi' (Chestnut-Leafed Oak), 'Kashiwa' (Daimyo Oak), etc.

Ichō (Maidenhair or Gingko Tree)

Characteristics 'Ichō' (Maidenhair or Gingko Tree) is one of the rare plants in the world in that it is a gymnospermous plant with only one species in one genus in one family. Some trees are over a thousand years old. It is well known for the fact that its pollen diffuses sperms that cause fertilization. It is extremely difficult to reproduce the aged appearance of this tree in a container in the form of *bonsai*, but it is comparatively easy to let it develop numerous stalactitic aerial roots seen only in large trees, or to make it bear nuts the size of cherries. The fan-shaped leaves of this tree turn yellow

in autumn and the sight is indeed beautiful. So it is considered one of the most outstanding specimens of *bonsai*.

If *bonsai* of 'Ichō' can be made successfully outside of Japan, as in the United States and elsewhere, it would, indeed, be a delightful surprise. And yet, it is not such a difficult task.

Material tree The material tree is grown from seedlings, cuttings, grafted trees, and trees obtained by root-grafting. With the use of seedlings, it is possible to view the yellow leaves of the tree from the second year. But if aerial roots are to be developed,

97

it takes at least thirty years of patient and hard labor. However, with the method of root-grafting, it is possible to have stalactitic aerial roots in about 4 to 5 years.

If the bearing of nuts is desired, a female tree must be obtained, as this is a monoecious plant, which has trees, male and female. If a female seedling is used, one has to wait about 20 years, but if the method of grafting is used, it can be obtained after two or three years.

'Ichō' has different kinds of leaves, large and small, and some have round nuts and others oblong. Some trees bear nuts in abundance while others do not. Some develop numerous stalactitic aerial roots and others only a few. So in selecting a material tree for *bonsai*, great care must be taken.

Some people are very desirous of developing an 'Ichō' *bonsai* which has beautiful yellow leaves, bearing many nuts and with numerous stalactitic aerial roots. Unfortunately, with the present technical knowledge, it is not possible to breed such an ideal *bonsai*. At present, there are two kinds: one with beautiful yellow leaves and stalactitic aerial roots, and one that bears nuts.

Growing care The soil for planting should be an equal mixture of black loam and red clay. There should be a layer of coarse sand at the bottom, and the soil should become finer as it nears the surface. This is necessary to ensure good water-drainage. After the planting, root-decay occurs rather easily until the roots develop. This can be prevented by not exposing the plant to heavy rain and by scanty watering.

The place for putting *bonsai,* and the watering technique are practically the same as for any other *bonsai.* However, in mid-summer, leaf-burn is a common occurrence. This jeopardizes the yellowing of the leaves in autumn, which can be prevented by placing the container where the sun shines for only two or three hours in the morning and is shady in the afternoon. Expose the plant to plenty of dew at night. In places where there is much dust and exhaust gas from automobiles, the leaves should be frequently syringed with water in mid-summer to clean the branches, trunk and leaves.

'Ichō' is a tree with great vitality. It responds well to large amounts of fertilizer. However, the fertilizer should not be too strong. Weak liquid fertilizer should be given frequently instead of water during the growing season and the cold season. Somewhat stronger solutions should be given once or twice.

If the purpose of the tree is to view the yellow leaves in autumn, apply rapeseed cake in liquid form. But if the nuts or stalactitic aerial roots are to be viewed, fish meal or bone meal should be applied.

The shape of the tree and arranging the branches 'Ichō' has the characteristic of growing into a huge tree reaching high up to the sky. So, even in the case of *bonsai,* it is wiser to develop a tree shape that resembles as much as possible its natural form. It therefore happens sometimes that the *bonsai* becomes very tall, over 60 cm. However, if the top is pinched every year in order to prevent the tree from growing too tall, and if the branches are made to grow dense in proportion to the height of the tree, it is possible to have a broom-shaped tree of dwarfed size.

Pinching All unnecessary new buds as well as those that have sprung from near the roots should be pulled off from the base immediately upon their appearance. The terminal buds should be pinched, leaving two or three leaves, when the leaves have more or less hardened. When the secondary buds appear, these, too, should be pinched, leaving two or three leaves out of four or five. New shoots which are necessary for making

into branches should be allowed to grow until the leaves have more or less hardened. Then only their tips should be pinched.

All other shoots should be pinched repeatedly, leaving two leaves out of three or four. However, after the second pinching, no more pinching should be done after the new twigs have hardened. The reason for this is that the places where cuts have been made will not heal properly, causing the branches to wither in winter.

Trimming the branches The branches should be trimmed in spring at the time of transplanting. Keeping balance with the overall appearance of the tree, cut the branches to the proper length, removing all unnecessary ones. In cutting off a branch, be sure to leave a healthy bud under each branch which has been cut.

Transplanting Transplanting is done once every spring when the new buds appear as dots of green. Sometimes coarse sand is mixed in the soil for planting, but too much of it will hamper the growth of the root system as well as invite a sparse branch growth. Using leaf mold instead of sand is recommended. The proportion should be 5 parts of red clay, 5 of black loam and 2 of leaf mold.

Arranging by wiring and leaf-cutting Neither of these operations should be done on 'Ichō'.

How to make the yellow leaves in autumn beautiful Place the plant where there is plenty of fresh air, and let the plant keep its thick green leaves until as late in autumn as possible.

How to make the plant bear numerous stalactitic aerial roots First select a material tree that belongs to the species that bears many stalactitic aerial roots. Everything else depends on growing and the patient care bestowed on the plant.

How to make the plant bear nuts First select a material tree that belongs to the strain that bears many nuts. Apply fertilizer rich in phosphate and potash in large quantities. The important thing is to leave the tree in the neighborhood of a tree that bears male flowers. However, as the pollen of 'Ichō' is very minute, it scatters like mist over a distance of more than 30 kilometers. Accordingly, if there are any trees bearing male flowers within this radius, a male tree in the neighborhood is not needed.

Beni-Shitan (Rock Cotoneaster)

Characteristics This is an evergreen shrub of a fairly hardy nature with numerous branches, which ramify into dense, smaller branches. The internodes are short and the branches do not grow too long. The dense leaves are small and thick, and have a sheen. It bears numerous flowers, and even a young tree bears small round berries that completely cover the branches. These berries ripen in late autumn and turn deep red.

They are particularly beautiful to look at in winter.

From the above description, it is easily to conceive that 'Beni-Shitan' is a plant particularly suited for growing as *bonsai*. It can be grown into any desired shape. Moreover, it is an easy plant to grow which a beginner can enjoy viewing while practising the technique of arranging by wiring.

Beni-Shitan (Rock Contoneaster)

Beni-Shitan (Rock Cotoneaster)

Material tree A material tree can be obtained either from a seedling, cutting, or a tree propagated by layering. Cuttings and trees propagated by layering have the advantage in that they develop roots quickly. And such trees bear berries sooner than trees obtained by other means. Accordingly, these two types of material trees are preferred.

Shapely trees, however, are very rare. Thus, such trees are quite expensive. On the contrary, unshapely trees are very common and can be purchased at no extra cost. So it is wise to purchase a cheap tree with a thick trunk and use only the better-shaped branches for purposes of layering. This is a quick way of getting a good 'Beni-Shitan' *bonsai*.

Layering The best time for layering is when the new buds begin to grow. Peel the bark around the place where you wish to cut off the branch, wrap the part with water-soaked sphagnum moss, and keep watering the moss so that it is always moist. After about three weeks, roots will develop. In two months, the branch is ready to be separated from the parent tree.

Growing The soil in which the plant is to be planted should be a mixture of 4 parts of black loam, 3 of red clay and 3 of coarse sand. The container should be an unglazed azalea pot. Plant the tree, making certain that water-drainage is good. And when the roots are firmly developed, place the container on an outdoor shelf to give it sufficient sunlight.

Give plenty of water. The leaves may be syringed with water in mid-summer after the leaves have hardened. For fertilizer, use liquid fertilizer consisting of rapeseed cake, mixed with fish meal or bone meal, or a small amount of superphosphate. Besides, deposit solid fertilizer on the soil. After the tree has borne berries, use rather strong liquid fertilizer three or four times until autumn; after that, there should be no further applications.

Pinching and branch-trimming Pinching in the case of 'Beni-Shitan' is similar to that of 'Umemodoki'. Long, over-grown branches, as well as unnecessary branches, should be trimmed in the following spring at the time of transplanting, so that the tree can be formed into a shapely appearance.

Wiring Wiring of the trunk and branches should be done in spring before the buds come out. When bending a trunk or a branch acutely, wrap the part with raffia, and use paper-wrapped wires. Paper-wrapped wires may be applied directly to new twigs.

Transplanting Transplanting should be done once every spring before the buds come out. And if the tree has developed wart-like swellings near the roots at that time, remove these warts, and disinfect with lime emulsion before transplanting.

Karin (Chinese Quince)

Characteristics Of all deciduous trees that are grown as *bonsai*, perhaps there is no other plant that is so hardy and long-lived as 'Karin'. The trunk is hard and the bark is smooth. The tree does not look so imposing when it is young, but as the tree grows older, it increases in grandeur. The bark develops spots which have a characteristic elegance. Hence, the bark alone is a sufficient source of enjoyment in itself. This can be said of the branches, too. As the branches increase in number, the tree puts on the appearance of a large tree. The leaves are rather large, and the tree does not bear many flowers, but the sight of the large elliptical yellow fruits that ripen on the branches after the leaves have fallen is one that pleases the eye of all. When these fruits are ripe, they emit a sweet fragrance. The tree is well suited for growing either as a *bonsai* with a single straight trunk, with a slanting trunk, or in semi-cascade style. The technique of growing is not so difficult, either. Some claim that the tree does not bear many fruits, but with proper fertilizer application and proper trimming of branches, it will bear many fruits.

Material tree 'Karin' is a plant that de-

Karin (Chinese Quince) of fruit being cultivated on a roof.

velops roots very well, so a material tree is generally obtained by layering. The technique of obtaining trees by layering is the same as for 'Beni-Shitan'. If the tree has a trunk or a branch with a diameter of 3 to 5 cm., it can be cut off after half a year and used as a material tree.

Growing The purpose of 'Karin' is to make it bear large fruits and enjoy viewing them. And to ensure the same, a good tree must be grown with a properly arranged tree shape.

The soil for planting should be a mixture of 4 parts of black loam, 3 of red clay, 2 of Kanuma soil, and 1 of coarse sand. The soil should hold and drain water well. Trim all unnecessary branches, and then plant firmly so that the tree will not move. The container should be placed where there is plenty of sunshine and air.

Since the plant has large leaves, it should always be given plenty of water. Lack of water must be avoided by all means. While the tree is young, the fertilizer required is rapeseed cake in weak liquid form, combined with solid fertilizer deposited on the soil. Both should be applied in sufficient quantities.

Pinching All unnecessary buds should be pinched as soon as they appear. As for the new buds that are needed to develop into branches, they should be allowed to grow until the leaves are more or less hardened. Then pinch just their tips. Other shoots to be developed into small branches should be stopped from growing after the height has reached 4 to 6 cm. So, the pinching should be delayed until the leaves have hardened to some extent, leaving just one or two leaves.

This causes the secondary buds to come out. These buds should be pinched like the first. Buds appearing for the third time should also be pinched.

If pinching is repeated in this way, 'Karin' which is a very vigorous tree will develop few branches and can be prevented from growing unnecessarily tall, with the increase of small branches. Dense young shoots should be thinned out in the process of pinching to arrange the branches properly.

Arranging the branches by wiring Arranging of the new twigs should be done with paper-wrapped wires at the time of pinching. In doing so, care should be taken not to snap the new twigs because the tree is soft and easily breakable during this time.

One-year old branches as well as two- to three-year old branches should be arranged by wiring with paper-wrapped wires in early spring just before the buds come out. It is better not to wire the old branches or the trunk. The wires should be removed in the autumn of the same year so as to prevent them from cutting into the bark.

Cold-proof measures 'Karin' is a strong cold resistant, but because it is often subjected to pinching, there is danger that the tips of the branches will wither in winter. Hence, the plant should be given a frost-proof shelter to provide protection against cold.

Trimming the branches Withered and overgrown branches may be trimmed in early spring before the buds come out, keeping harmony and balance with the tree shape. Thick branches should not be cut off at one stroke. Such branches should be cut off over a period of two or three years, cutting them a little shorter every year.

Transplanting Transplanting should be done once in spring every year, before the buds come out. Compared with other deciduous trees, 'Karin' puts out buds earlier in spring. So it is important not to do it at the wrong time. The tree is so vigorous that its roots fill the container in one year. Therefore, in transplanting, the roots should be pruned close.

Fertilizing to stimulate fruit-bearing After the tree has grown to have a more or less definite shape, rapeseed cake alone is not sufficient as nutrient. Weak liquid fertilizer consisting of bone meal or fish bones or a small amount of superphosphate should be added. Fertilizer should be deposited on the soil from time to time. Also, in order to make up for the potash deficiency during the growing season, it is effective to give a solution of wood ash now and then.

However, no fertilizer should be applied during the flowering season and after the formation of fruits. Watering is sufficient during this period.

Relation between pinching and the bearing of fruits It is necessary to pinch buds repeatedly. In the case of other deciduous trees, repeated pinching generally jeopardizes the proper development of branches. Consequently, no formation of flower-buds takes place. If the blossoms are poor, naturally the fruits will be inferior. However, 'Karin' is an exception, in that, with sufficient fertilizer application, pinching can be repeated several times without any ill effects.

Picking the fruits and cautions to be observed in summer 'Karin' is a tree that bears large fruits. If it is allowed to bear too many fruits at one time, the tree becomes exhausted and will not bear any fruits the next year. Therefore, when the tree has put on a large number of fruits, they should be examined when they have become as large as nuts, and leaving two or three that are well-developed and in good positions, thin out the rest.

If the fruits that have been left are exposed to the strong afternoon sun in mid-summer, sunburn results, and the part which is exposed to the sun becomes black. The fruits may even drop off before they are fully developed. So the tree should not be exposed to the afternoon sun in mid-summer.

Again, if the ripened fruits are left on the tree until they drop, the tree loses its vitality. They should be picked off the tree at a suitable time.

Bonsai being cultivated on a roof.

BRIEF DESCRIPTION OF THE GROWING TECHNIQUE OF *BONSAI*

Needle-Leafed Evergreens.

'Aka-Matsu' (Japanese Red Pine)
(Time for transplanting) Once every three or four years in spring after the appearance of the buds.
(Soil) 70% red clay and 30% coarse sand.
(Watering) Not too much watering. Leaves should be syringed during mid-summer.
(Fertilizer) Deposit fertilizer of rapeseed cake about three times during the growing season.
(Pinching) Same as in the case of 'Kuro-Matsu' (Japanese Black Pine).
(Arranging by wiring) Same as in the case of 'Kuro-Matsu' (Japanese Black Pine).
(Other points to bear in mind) Pick off old leaves by hand after mid-summer. Trim all unnecessary branches at the time of transplanting.

'Kara-Matsu' (Japanese Larch)
(Time for transplanting) Once every three or four years in spring before the sprouting of the buds.
(Soil) 50% red clay and 50% coarse sand.
(Watering) Take care to apply the right amount of water. Give plenty of water right after transplanting, during the spring

Aka-Matsu (Japanese Red Pine)
Seedling tree.

Kara-Matsu (Japanese Larch)

budding season and in mid-summer.

(Fertilizer) Avoid giving excessive fertilizer by all means. Deposit fertilizer consisting of rapeseed cake twice during the growth of new twigs.

(Pinching) Wait until side-buds appear next to the new twigs, then pinch the buds when these new twigs have grown too long, leaving one or two side-buds.

(Arranging by wiring) Avoid wiring the trunk or thick branches, as the bark is soft and because of the danger that the wires might cut into the tree. New twigs to be grown into branches and to be arranged should be wired with paper-wrapped wire.

(Other points to bear in mind) Take cold proof measures in winter. Prune all unnecessary branches at the time of transplanting. Do not let the roots molder.

'Kome-Tsuga' (Japanese Northern Hemlock)

(Time for transplanting) Once every three or four years during the spring budding time.

(Soil) 40 to 50% red clay and 60 to 50% coarse sand.

(Watering) Little watering is needed, but the leaves should be syringed thoroughly during budding time and in summer.

(Fertilizer) Very weak liquid fertilizer should be applied two or three times in spring at budding-time. After that, rapeseed may be deposited about twice during the growing season.

(Pinching) The buds should be pinched once when the leaves are more or less hardened.

(Wiring) Bare wire may be applied in spring, but avoid strong wiring.

(Other points to bear in mind) Unnecessary branches should be trimmed at the time of wiring.

'Onko' (Japanese Yew) and 'Kaya' (Torrela nucifera)

Both of these plants may be treated in the same ways as 'Kome-Tsuga' (Japanese Northern Hemlock). However, 'Onko' (Japanese Yew) dislikes a strong sunshine, so in summer, keep it out of strong sunshine.

'Hinoki' (Hinoki Cypress) and 'Tsukumo-Hiba' (Dwarf Form of Sawara Cypress)

(Time for transplanting) Once every other year, preferably in early spring.

(Soil) 50% black loam, 20% leaf mold, and 30% coarse sand.

(Watering) Give plenty of water. Leaves need practically no watering.

(Fertilizer) The same kind of fertilizer may be used as for 'Shimpaku' (Chinese Juniper).

(Pinching) Pinch the buds with the fingers in spring and autumn when new buds come out vigorously. Twice in spring and once in autumn should be enough.

(Arranging by wiring) Wiring should be done in early spring.

(Other points to bear in mind) Unnecessary branches should be pruned in autumn in warm climates, while in other climates, at thte time of arranging by wiring.

'Sawara' (Sawara Cypress)

Method used for 'Hinoki' (Hinoki Cypress) can be applied with some modification. However, for fertilizer, liquid fertilizer is preferable. In summer, syringe the leaves.

'Konote-Kashiwa' (Chinese Arborvitae)

(Transplanting) Once every two or three years, preferably in early spring.

(Soil) 50% red clay, 20% black loam, and 30% coarse sand.

(Watering) Do not water too much during any period. In summer, expose the plant to all possible dew at night.

(Fertilizer) Deposit fertilizer consisting of rapeseed cake three to four times during the growing season.

(Pinching) Pinching should be done three times a year, same as in the case of 'Hinoki' (Hinoki Cypress).

(Arranging by wiring) As the branches and leaves of 'Konote-Kashiwa' (Chinese Arborvitae) have a tendency to grow straight and hand-shaped, wiring with bare wire should be carried out in early spring before budding time in order to change the distribution of the branches and leaves so as to arrange the shape of the tree.

(Other points to bear in mind) This is a

very hardy tree and is able to withstand extreme heat and cold as well as dryness.

However, it is susceptible to dampness.

Deciduous Trees—Flowering Trees

'Rōbai' (Beeswax Flower)

(Time for transplanting)   Once a year, or once in every two years, after the flowering season.

(Soil)   60% black loam, 30% Kanuma soil, and 10% coarse sand.

(Giving water)   Watering should be the same as for 'Ume' (Flowering Japanese Apricot).

(Fertilizer)   As in the case of 'Ume' (Flowering Japanese Apricot), use a weak liquid fertilizer with organic fertilizer.

(Pinching)   Pinch off all unnecessary new buds as soon as they appear. New shoots should be trimmed in mid-summer as seems fit.

(Arranging by wiring)   Wiring of old branches is a difficult task. Paper-wrapped wires should be used for new twigs.

(Other points to bear in mind)   As 'Rōbai' (Beeswax Flower) is weak in cold resistance, it should be taken indoors in early winter. Prune the branches to an appropriate length, carefully observing the condition of the flower buds in late autumn or early spring. When transplanting, take care not to prune the roots too closely. In summer, do not expose the plant to the strong afternoon sun.

'Ōbai' (Winter Jasmine)

(Time for transplanting)   Once a year, either in autumn after the leaves have fallen, or in spring before the flowers bloom.

(Soil)   Practically the same as for 'Rōbai' (Beeswax flower).

Obai (Winter Jasmine)

(Watering) Expose the plant to plenty of sunshine all the time and water the roots sufficiently upon drying.

(Fertilizer) Use liquid fertilizer after the flowering season until autumn. The best fertilizer is rapeseed cake mixed with bone meal or a small amount of superphosphate.

(Pinching) Pinch off all unnecessary new shoots before they become large. New shoots which have been left should be allowed to grow long, and then cut to a suitable length when the lower portions of the new twigs begin to harden.

(Arranging by wiring) Paper-wrapped wires should be used after pinching.

(Other points to bear in mind) 'Ōbai' (Winter Jasmine) has a tendency to root from its nodes. So, all roots springing from the branches must be cut off as soon as possible. Overgrown branches should be cut to a suitable length before the flowering-season according to the condition to the flower-buds.

'Sanzashi' (Chinese Hawthorn)

(Time for transplanting) Once in spring before the sprouting of the buds.

(Soil) 60% black loam, 20% red clay, and 20% coarse sand.

(Watering) Give plenty of watering.

(Fertilizer) Apply weak liquid fertilizer twice a month during the growing season. However, in the case of trees that bear berries, apply rather strong liquid fertilizer containing phosphate and potash in the second half of the period.

(Pinching) Pinch off the tips of the shoots when the leaves of the new buds have begun to harden.

(Arranging by wiring) Use paper-wrapped wires when the new shoots have begun to harden. The wires should be removed in autumn.

(Other points to bear in mind) The branches should be pruned either after the flowers or after viewing the berries. A plant with too many berries should be thinned out before the berries fall naturally, otherwise the tree becomes weak.

'Kaido (Showy Crab Apple)

(Time for transplanting) Once in spring before the sprouting of the buds.

(Soil) 70% black loam, 10% Kanuma soil, and 20% coarse sand.

(Watering) Give plenty of water.

(Fertilizer) As in the case of 'Sanzashi' (Chinese Hawthorn), there are two kinds of 'Kaidō' (Showy Crab Apple), one for the enjoyment of the flowers, the other for the enjoyment of the fruits. The method of fertilizer application is the same as for 'Sanzashi' (Chinese Hawthorn).

(Pinching) The new buds should be pinched at the tips after being allowed to grow.

(Arranging by wiring) Paper-wrapped wires should be used about the time the new shoots begin to harden.

(Other points to bear in mind) A tree that has borne a large number of fruits must have these fruits picked after enjoying them for some time, otherwise the tree will become weak. Large scars on the branches or trunk should be carved in winter, and sphagnum moss tied to the place. This hastens the healing process.

'Sakura' (Flowering Cherry)

(Time for transplanting) Once every spring before the sprouting of the buds.

(Soil) The soil should be a mixture of black loam, red clay, and coarse sand in equal proportion.

(Watering) Do not water too much, except in the case of the alpine 'Fuji-Zakura (Prumus incisa), which requires syringing on the leaves at intervals.

(Fertilizer) This tree is weak in fertilizer resistance, so organic fertilizer should be avoided. The best fertilizer is very weak liquid fertilizer consisting of rapeseed cake, applied several times during the growing season.

(Pinching) Trim the branches after the flowering-season, leaving two or three nodes. As for the new buds, pinch off their tips about the time the leaves have more or less hardened.

(Arranging by wiring) Paper-wrapped wires should be used at the time of bud-pinching. These wires should be removed in autumn.

(Other points to bear in mind) All unnecessary branches should be trimmed at

Sakura (Flowering Cherry)

the time of transplanting. However, do not tamper too much with the branches. Eradicate insects immediately upon discovery.

'Mokuren' (Lily Magnolia) and 'Kobushi' (Kobushi Magnolia)

(Time for transplanting)   Once a year, immediately after the flowering season.

(Soil)   60% black loam, 20–30% red clay, and 10–20% coarse sand.

(Watering)   Give plenty of water. Place the container in summer in a cool, shady place exposing it to the sunshine for about two or three hours in the morning.

(Fertilizer)   Fertilizer application should be concentrated on the first half of the growing season.   Liquid fertilizer should be applied two or three times a month.

(Pinching)   This is a tree with few ramifications.   Accordingly, clip off only those new buds which are unnecessary, and the new buds which have been left should be pinched to a suitable length when the leaves have hardened.

(Arranging by wiring)   Paper-wrapped wires should be used at the time of pinching, removing the wires in autumn.

(Other points to bear in mind)   The flowers have a tendency to bloom with their backs to the sun.   So the container should be moved now and then.

'Zaifuriboku' (Japanese Juneberry)

(Time for transplanting)   Once a year in spring before the sprouting of the buds.

(Soil)   50% black loam, 30% red clay, 10% leaf mold, and 10% coarse sand.

(Watering)   Water the leaves in spring when the buds sprout. Afterwards, give plenty of water during the growing season.

(Fertilizer)   Apply liquid fertilizer twice a month during the growing season.   During the first half of the season, use very weak fertilizer and during the second half, make the fertilizer gradually stronger. However, give it less frequently.

(Pinching)   Trim the branches after the flowering season.   Let the new buds grow until the leaves harden somewhat, then pinch their tips.

(Other points to bear in mind) This is a tree with few ramifications. So do not prune the branches too close.

'Zakuro' (Pomegranate)

(Time for transplanting) Once a year, or once every two years, about the time when the new buds have begun to open their new leaves in spring.

(Soil) 50% black loam, 10% leaf mold, 20% Kanuma soil, and 20% coarse sand.

(Watering) Water drainage must be good when the tree is planted. Expose to plenty of sunshine. It may be left outdoors even in summer. Give plenty of water. Expose to the dew at night.

(Fertilizer) Use decomposed liquid fertilizer consisting of rapeseed cake mixed with bone meal or fish-bones. During the first half of the growing season, apply weak fertilizer three to four times a month, and during the second half, gradually stronger fertilizer twice a month.

(Pinching) Pinch the new shoots when they reach a height of 9 to 12 cm., leaving 1 to 2 nodes. The secondary buds should be pinched off when they reach a height of 7 to 8 cm., leaving one node.

(Arranging by wiring) Use paper-wrapped wires at the time of pinching once every other year.

(Other points to bear in mind) Too many flower-buds at the tips of new twigs should be thinned out. The fruits which have grown should be plucked off before they fall off naturally so as to prevent the tree from becoming weak.

'Sarusuberi' (Crape Myrtle)

(Time for transplanting) Once every spring around budding-time.

(Soil) 80% black loam and 20% coarse sand.

(Watering) The roots should be watered the same as for any other plant. The leaves should be watered during budding-time.

(Fertilizer) As the plant is slow in sprouting buds and is quick in losing leaves, sufficient liquid fertilizer as well as organic manure should be applied from the time it has developed roots until mid-summer.

(Pinching) The branches should be pruned close before the sprouting of the buds. The new buds should be pinched at the time the flower-buds begin to sprout and also after the flowering-season.

(Arranging by wiring) Use paper-wrapped wires during mid-summer.

(Other points to bear in mind) The tree will not bear many flowers when pinched too early and too often. Give cold protection in winter.

'Nemu-no-ki' (Silk Tree)

(Time for transplanting) Once every two years before the sprouting of the buds in spring.

(Soil) 50% black loam, 20% red clay, 10% leaf mold, and 20% coarse sand.

(Watering) Water plentifully. In summer, place the plant in a place where the sun shines for about two or three hours in the morning and then becomes shady afterwards. Expose the plant to the dew at night.

(Fertilizer) Apply liquid fertilizer once every ten days or so during the growing season. Some wood ash solution should be added to liquid fertilizer now and then.

(Pinching) The new twigs should not be pinched too close. Pinch the tips of the buds only to the extent that the shape of the tree is not ruined.

(Arranging by wiring) The method is the same as for 'Sarusuberi' (Crape Myrtle).

(Other points to bear in mind) The branches should be trimmed at the time of transplanting and also after the flowering-season. In winter give cold protection.

Evergreen Trees—Flowering Trees

'Tsubaki' (Camellias)

(Time for transplanting) In the case of

a tree that is still young, transplanting should be done once every two years, and for a mature tree with completed shape, once every three years. The best time is after the flowering-season, whether it is a variety that blooms in winter or in spring. However, no transplanting should be done during the cold weather in winter.

(Soil) 70% black loam, 30% red clay, and 20% coarse sand.

(Watering) Watering should be the same as for any other plant. Avoid exposure to the strong afternoon sun during the period from the hardening of the leaves until summer. Water the leaves frequently.

(Fertilizer) If only liquid fertilizer is to be applied during the growing season, apply it twice a month. During the second half of the same season, add some phosphate and potash in somewhat large quantities. Sufficient fertilizer should be applied to a young tree.

(Pinching) The tips of the shoots should be pinched off when the leaves have somewhat hardened. Trim the tips of the branches after the flower-buds have formed.

(Arranging by wiring) Use paper-wrapped wires at the time of pinching.

(Other points to bear in mind) Too many flower-buds should be thinned out. The branches should be pruned at the time of transplanting. The plant should be kept indoors in winter where there is plenty of light.

'Satsuki' (Satsuki Azalea)

(Time for transplanting) Young trees should be transplanting once every year; older trees once every two years. In both cases, the best time is after the flowering-season.

(Soil) 60 to 70% Kanuma soil, mixed with 40 to 30% sphagnum moss shredded fine.

(Giving water) Expose the plant to plenty of sunshine with good watering on the roots. Moreover, the leaves should be syringed right after transplanting until the plant develops roots as well as every morning and evening in summer. Place the container in a cool place in summer and keep it out of the direct sun.

(Fertilizer) Except during the flowering-season, use weak liquid fertilizer two or three times a month during the growing season.

(Pinching) Pinch all unnecessary buds immediately upon their sprouting. As for overgrown new shoots, pinch them off while they are still soft, leaving two or three leaves.

(Arranging by wiring) Wiring should be carried out during the growing season. Wrap raffia first around the trunk and thick branches and use paper-wrapped wires.

(Other points to bear in mind) Trim all withered branches and those that have grown too dense at the time of transplanting and also at the time of arranging by wiring. Too many flower-buds should be thinned out. After the flowering season is over, cut off all withered flowers to prevent the bearing of seeds.

'Kuchinashi' (Cape Gardenia)

(Time for transplanting) Once every year in spring before the appearance of the buds.

(Soil) 50% black loam, 30% red clay, and

(Giving water) Expose the plant to sufficient sunlight. Give a small amount of water.

(Fertilizer) During the growing season, apply weak liquid fertilizer consisting of rapeseed cake and organic fertilizer twice a month.

(Pinching) Pinch off the tips of the shoots when the leaves on the new twigs have hardened. Overgrown branches and withered branches should be pruned at the time of transplanting.

(Arranging by wiring) Use paper-wrapped wires at the time of pinching.

(Other points to bear in mind) Place the container in semi-shade during the summer and give cold protection in winter. Cut off the fruits before they dry and wither.

'Haze' (Japanese Wax Tree)

(Time for transplanting) Once every year in spring just prior to the sprouting of the buds.

(Soil) 50% black loam soil, 20% red clay, 20% leaf mold, and 10% coarse sand.

(Watering) Watering should be the same as for any other tree, but not too much. Syringe the leaves in mid-summer.

(Fertilizer) Apply fertilizer mostly during the first half of the growing season. Use liquid fertilizer about twice a month.

(Pinching) When the new shoots have fully grown, pinch the shoots, leaving two or three leaves.

(Arranging by wiring) Use paper-wrapped wires on new twigs in summer, and to older branches in spring before the buds come out.

(Other points to bear in mind) In summer, do not expose the plant to the afternoon sun and give cold protection in winter.

'Nishikigi' (Winged Spindle Tree) and 'Mayumi' (Japanese Strawberry Bush)

(Time for transplanting) Once every spring about the time the buds sprout.

(Soil) Same as for 'Haze' (Japanese Wax Tree).

(Watering) Watering should be the same as for any other plant. In summer, place the container in semi-shade, and water the leaves frequently.

(Fertilizer) Since the purpose of the plant is to enjoy its autumnal tints as well as its berries, use liquid fertilizer consisting of rapeseed cake mixed with bone meal or a small amount of superphosphate. Use the same in weak solution during the first half of the growing season, applying it three times a month. During the second half of the same season, make the solution somewhat stronger and apply it twice a month or so.

(Pinching) Pinch off the new shoots, leaving about two buds. Overgrown branches as well as unnecessary branches should be trimmed at the time of transplanting.

(Arranging by wiring) Use paper-wrapped wires at the time of pinching.

(Other points to bear in mind) Large or soiled leaves should be cut off just before mid-summer.

'Megi' (Japanese Berberry)

(Time for transplanting) Once every spring at the time of budding.

(Soil) 50% black loam, 30% red clay, and 20% coarse sand.

(Watering) Give plenty of water. In summer, place the plant in semi-shade, syringe the leaves frequently.

(Fertilizer) The purpose of this plant is to enjoy its autumnal tints and also its berries, so apply fertilizer the same as for 'Nishikigi' mentioned above.

(Pinching) Pinching should be done two or three times. The flowers of this plant appear at the sides of the leaves on the new twigs. So the new shoots should be allowed to grow fairly long before they are trimmed.

(Arranging by wiring) At the time of transplanting, first cut off all unnecessary branches and then use paper-wrapped wires.

(Other points to bear in mind) In handling, look out for the sharp thorns.

'Tsuta' (Japanese Ivy)

(Time for transplanting) Once every spring before the sprouting of the buds.

(Soil) 70% red clay, 20% Kanuma soil, and 10% coarse sand.

(Watering) Give plenty of water. Syringe the leaves in summer frequently.

(Fertilizer) During the first half of the growing season, use weak liquid fertilizer three times a month.

(Pinching) As 'Tsuta' (Japanese Ivy), is a climbing plant, cut the vines, leaving each of two leaves, whenever they have reached height of 6 to 9 cm. to prevent overgrowth.

(Arranging by wiring) Use paper-wrapped wires at the time of transplanting. Old branches cannot be bent acutely as they are brittle and tend to snap easily.

(Other points to bear in mind) Cut off all small vines immediately upon becoming too dense. Prune all unnecessary or withered branches at the time of transplanting.

'Shirakaba' (Japanese White Birch)

(Time for transplanting) Once every spring before the sprouting of the buds.

(Soil) 60% black loam, 20% red clay, and

20% coarse sand.

(Watering) Plant the tree in a good water-draining container, then give plenty of water. In summer, place the plant in semi-shade. Give the leaves plenty of water.

(Fertilizer) Fertilizer application should be concentrated on the first half of the growing season. Use very weak decayed liquid fertilizer, consisting of rapeseed cake mixed with bone meal two or three times a month.

(Pinching) As soon as the new shoots have grown, leave two or three leaves and pinch their buds once or twice.

(Arranging by wiring) Use paper-wrapped wires when the leaves on the new twigs have somewhat hardened. Remove these wires in autumn.

(Other points to bear in mind) Remove the soiled surface of the old bark once every two years. Do not use fertilizer with strong nitrogen.

'Yanagi' (Weeping Willow)

(Time for transplanting) Twice a year, in early summer and in mid-summer.

(Soil) 50% black loam, 30% Kanuma soil, and 20% coarse sand.

(Watering) 'Yanagi' (Weeping Willow) must be given a lot of water. In summer, place the container in cool semi-shade.

Keep the plant out of strong sunlight, especially the afternoon sun. Syringe the leaves frequently.

(Fertilizer) Give very weak liquid fertilizer three times a month during the growing season.

(Trimming the new shoots) Leave two or three nodes and prune the new shoots when the tree is transplanted. All new buds which then appear should be allowed to grow without pinching.

(Arranging by of wiring) 'Yanagi' (Weeping Willow) will soon start to sprout buds again vigorously after the new long grown shoots are pruned short. Accordingly, wiring should be applied only to the thick branches in early spring before the buds come out. Wires should be wrapped with paper before using.

(Other points to bear in mind) Do not delay the second transplanting. To prevent drying, the container may be put under water. If too long, it may cause oxygen shortage and root suffocation.

'Gyoryu' (Tamarisk)

(Time for transplanting) Once every spring about the time the buds sprout.

(Soil) The same as for 'Yanagi' (Weeping Willow).

(Watering and fertilizer) The same as for 'Yanagi' (Weeping Willow).

(Trimming the branches) Trim all branches close at the time of transplanting, keeping balance with the overall tree shape. Dense young shoots should be thinned out.

(Arranging by wiring) Use paper-wrapped wires for thick branches. In place of wiring, the method of suspending the branches might be employed.

(Other points to bear in mind) The important thing here is to distribute the young shoots properly. To ensure good shoot distribution, wiring is one method.

Deciduous Trees—Those That Bear Fruits

'Yusura-Ume' (Prunus tomentosa)

(Time for transplanting) Once every spring before the sprouting of the buds.

(Soil) The same as for 'Sanzashi' (Nippon Hawthorn).

(Watering) Expose the plant to plenty of sunshine. Give plenty of water, the same as for any other plant.

(Fertilizer) As the purpose is the enjoyment of the flowers as well as fruits, use weak liquid fertilizer consisting of rapeseed cake mixed with bone meal, applied two or three times a month during the growing season.

(Pinching) Pinch off the tops of the buds of the new overgrown shoots. In spring, at the time of transplanting prune the twigs to a suitable length, appropriately in relation to the condition of the flower-buds.

(Arranging by wiring) Use paper-wrapped wires for young branches before the appearance of the buds.

(Other points to bear in mind) One way to develop a young tree is to thin out the fruits by plucking them off. The plant has very weak resistance to chemical preparations. So care should be taken in the application of insecticide. Give the plant cold protection in winter.

'Kaki' (Japanese Persimmon)

(Time for transplanting) Once every year in spring before the appearance of the buds.

(Soil) 40% black loam, 30% red clay, 20% leaf mold, and 10% coarse sand.

(Watering) Expose the plant to sufficient sunlight, and give plenty of water, the same as for any other plant.

(Fertilizer) Use both liquid fertilizer and organic fertilizer during the growing season. During the second half of the same season, use fertilizer somewhat rich in phosphate and potash.

(Pinching) Pinch off all unnecessary young shoots as soon as possible. The flower-buds must be trimmed to a suitable length after their appearance on the new twigs.

(Arranging by wiring) Use paper-wrapped wires in order to arrange the branches when the leaves have somewhat hardened. Remove the wires in autumn.

(Other points to bear in mind) Give cold protection in winter. Give the tree a rest once every three years by not allowing it to bear any fruits. Prune the branches at the time of transplanting.

'Kuri' (Japanese Chestnut)

(Time for transplanting) Once every spring before the sprouting of the buds.

(Soil) 60% black loam, 20% Kanuma soil, and 20% coarse sand.

(Watering) Give plenty of water.

(Fertilizer) Apply weak liquid fertilizer consisting of rapeseed cake mixed with bone meal two or three times a month during the growing season.

(Pinching) Pinch the tips of the young shoots that tend to grow too long. Pinch the tips of the branches of the young twigs after the fruits have formed.

(Arranging by wiring) Use paper-wrapped wires for young shoots that are still tender.

(Other points to bear in mind) In winter, give cold protection to. prevent the branches from withering.

'Hime-Ringo' (Nagasaki Crab Apple)

(Time for transplanting) Once every spring around budding-time.

(Soil) 40% black loam, 20% red clay, 30% Kanuma soil, and 10% coarse sand.

(Giving water) Give water the same as for any other plant.

(Fertilizer) During the first half of the growing season apply weak liquid fertilizer, consisting of rapeseed cake mixed with bone meal or fish manure. During the second half, after the fruits have begun to grow large, use stronger liquid fertilizer, decreasing the number of applications.

(Pinching) Pinch off the tips of the shoots after some growth. The branches should be trimmed at the time of transplanting.

(Arranging by wiring) Use paper-wrapped wires at the time of pinching.

(Other points to bear in mind) The tree bears numerous fruits. So, after enjoying the view for some time, pluck them off to prevent the tree from becoming weak.

'Akebi' (Five-Leaf Akebia)

(Time for transplanting) Once every year, or once every two years, in spring at the appearance of the buds.

(Soil) 40% black loam, 30% red clay, 10% leaf mold, and 20% coarse sand.

(Watering) Give plenty of water. Do not expose the plant to the direct sun in summer, and syringe the leaves now and then.

(Fertilizer) Use liquid fertilizer mixed with organic manure. After the fruits have grown large, use somewhat stronger fertilizer.

(Pinching) Pinch off all unnecessary new shoots as soon as they appear. Overgrown shoots should be checked from further growth by being pulled down.

(Arranging by wiring) There is no need

Hime-Ringo (Nagasaki Crab Apple)

for this treatment.

(Other points to bear in mind) In order to make the plant bear many fruits, pollinate artificially. During the time between the opening of the flowers and the formation of the fruits, place the container in a place where there is not too much wind.

Evergreens—Those That Bear Fruits.

'Busshukan' (Fleshy-Fingered Citron)

(Time for transplanting) Once a year or once every two years, in spring around budding-time.

(Soil) 50% red clay, 30% black loam, and 20% coarse sand.

(Watering) Expose the plant to sufficient sunlight, and always give plenty of water.

(Fertilizer) Apply plenty of very weak liquid fertilizer consisting of fish manure or mixed with bone meal until the time the flowers open. This fertilizer should be applied instead of water. After the fruits have begun to grow large give somewhat stronger fertilizer twice a month and continue this until the fruits take on a faint color.

(Pinching) Trim the young shoots, leaving each of two leaves. As for the secondary shoots, pinch off their tips in autumn.

(Arranging by wiring) Arrange the branches by wiring whenever the buds are pinched. In doing so, wrap raffia around the old branches.

(Other points to bear in mind) Place the plant indoors, in winter to give cold protection. In order to thicken the branches pluck off the fruits early and apply plenty of fertilizer.